The MAILBOX®

The Education Center®

Renee

P9-BIK-330

PreK-K

Everything Numbers

Timesaving tools for teaching numbers 0–20

- **Counting**
- **One-to-one correspondence**
- **Number recognition**
- **Comparing sets**

  and more!

Develops number sense and mathematical thinking!

Managing Editor: Kelly Robertson

Editorial Team: Becky S. Andrews, Diane Badden, Kimberley Bruck, Karen A. Brudnak, Kitty Campbell, Pam Crane, Lynette Dickerson, Tazmen Hansen, Marsha Heim, Lori Z. Henry, Debra Liverman, Dorothy C. McKinney, Thad H. McLaurin, Sharon Murphy, Jennifer Nunn, Mark Rainey, Greg D. Rieves, Hope Rodgers, Eliseo De Jesus Santos II, Donna K. Teal, Zane Williard

www.themailbox.com

©2008 The Mailbox® Books
All rights reserved.
ISBN10 #1-56234-830-2 • ISBN13 #978-156234-830-4

Manufactured in the United States
10 9 8 7 6 5 4 3 2 1

What's

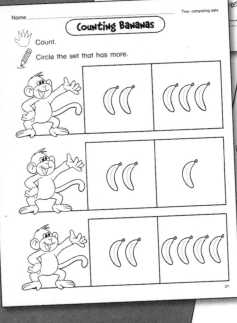

number illustrations

fun practice pages

fold-and-go booklets

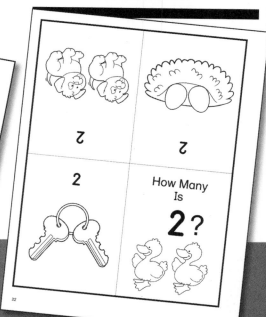

Inside

multipurpose number cards

12 ★★★★★★
★★★★★★
★★ twelve

illustrated number rhymes

8 mice
on the ice

a counting center

3 How Many Bees?

number games

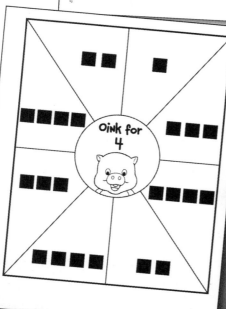

Oink for
4

Find 16
more ways to
use the teaching tools!
See page 169.

Table of Contents

What's Inside 2

Numbers

0 5

1 13

2 21

3 29

4 37

5 45

6 53

7 61

8 69

9 77

10 85

11 93

12 97

13 101

14 105

15 109

16 113

17 117

18 121

19 125

20 129

Number Cards 0–20 133

Number Rhymes 0–20 144

Counting Center 0–20 166

Bonus Activities 169

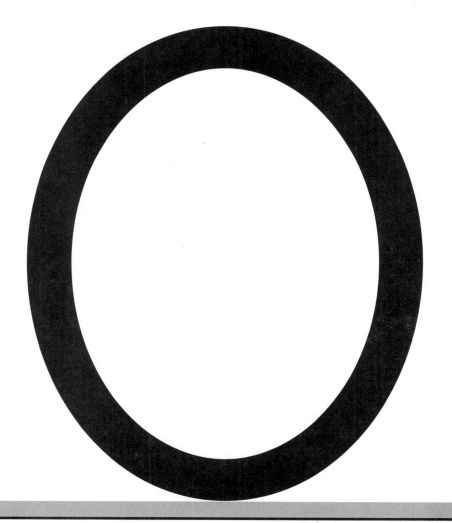

zero

O

O

How Many
Is
O ?

Everything Numbers • ©The Mailbox® Books • TEC61111

Fold-and-Go Booklet: To make a booklet, cut on the bold line. Fold along the thin horizontal line (keeping the programming to the outside) and then fold along the thin vertical line (keeping the cover to the outside).

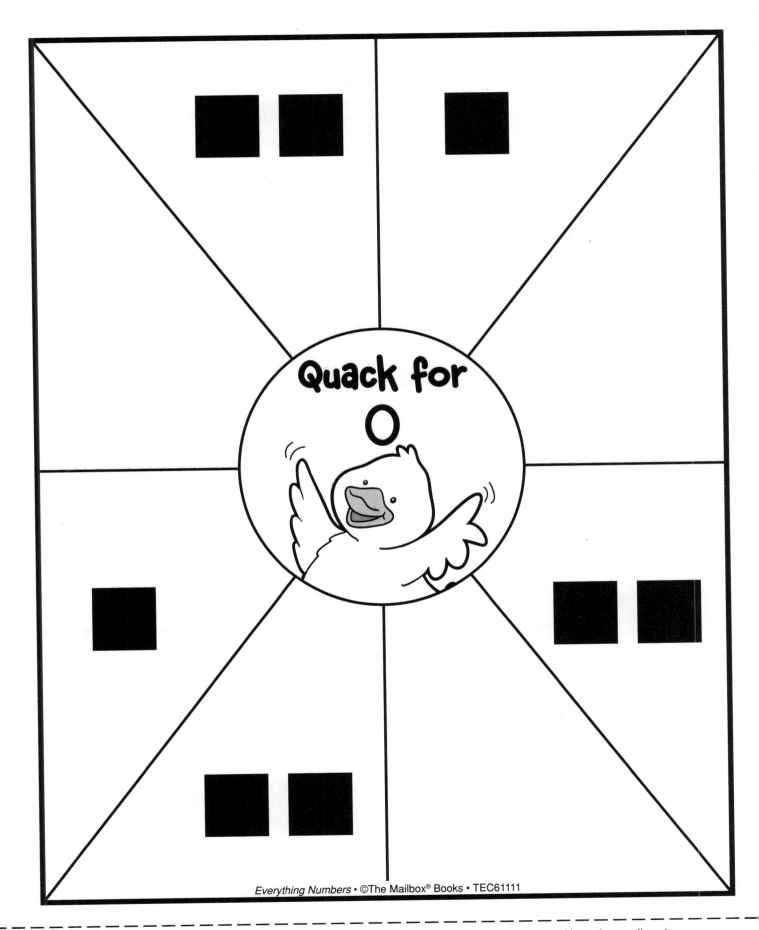

Quack for
0

Counting Game: Give each player a game strip from page 8 and a crayon. Players also need a pom-pom. Have players alternate tossing the pom-pom onto the gameboard. A player counts the squares in the game space where the pom-pom lands. When the pom-pom lands in the center circle or on a game space with zero squares, the player says "zero" and quacks; then she traces a 0 on her game strip. Play continues until one player traces all her numbers or until game time is over.

7

Quack!

Quack!

Quack!

Everything Numbers • ©The Mailbox® Books • TEC61111

Game Strips: Use with "Quack for 0" on page 7.

Zero Bunnies

 Color each 🧺 that has 0.

Name _____

Number Zero Train

Trace.

Cut.

Glue.

Everything Numbers • ©The Mailbox® Books • TEC61111

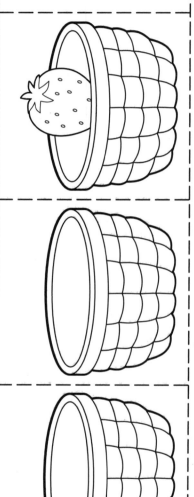

Note to the teacher: Have the child trace the numeral 0. Next, have her cut out the pictures and glue on the train each picture that shows zero items in the basket.

Counting Chicks

Count.

Circle the set that has more.

Name_____

Zeros Only

🖍 Color.

2	O	O	O	O	3
3	O	3	2	O	1
2	O	5	1	O	1
3	O	1	4	O	2
2	O	O	O	O	2

Everything Numbers • ©The Mailbox® Books • TEC61111

Note to the teacher: Have the child color each grid space that shows a numeral 0.

one

I

I

I

How Many
Is
I?

Fold-and-Go Booklet: To make a booklet, cut on the bold line. Fold along the thin horizontal line (keeping the programming to the outside) and then fold along the thin vertical line (keeping the cover to the outside).

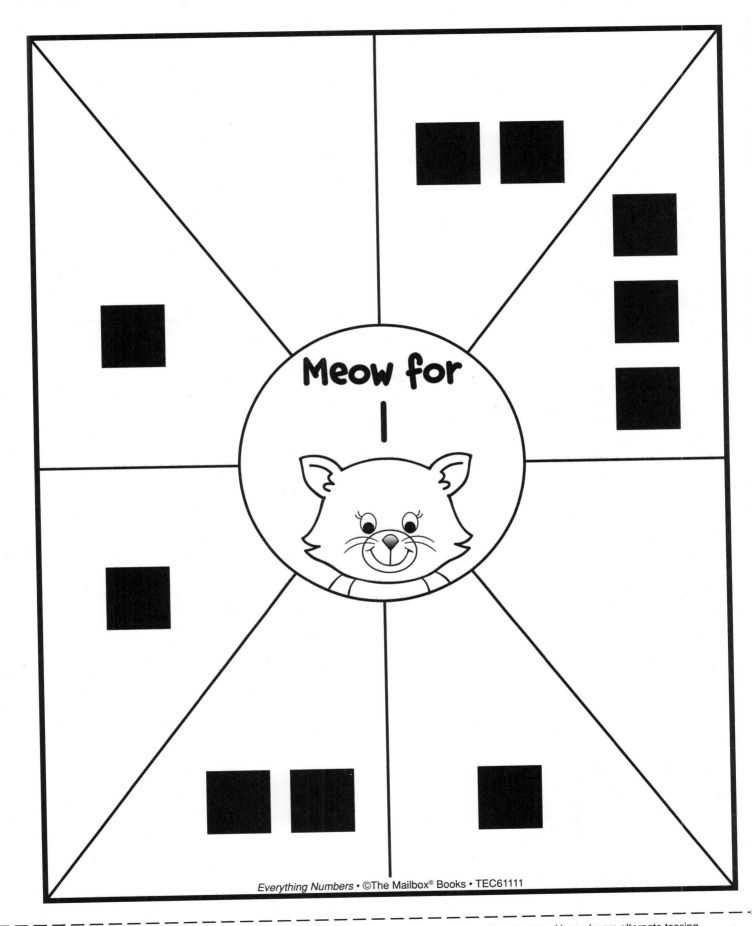

Meow for
1

Counting Game: Give each player a game strip from page 16 and a crayon. Players also need a pom-pom. Have players alternate tossing the pom-pom onto the gameboard. A player counts the squares in the game space where the pom-pom lands. When the pom-pom lands in the center circle or on a game space with one square, the player says "one" and meows; then he traces a 1 on his game strip. Play continues until one player traces all his numbers or until game time is over.

Meow!

TEC61111

Meow!

TEC61111

Meow!

Everything Numbers • ©The Mailbox® Books • TEC61111

One Fish

Color each 🐟 that has 1.

Name _____

18

Number One Train

Trace.

Cut.

Glue.

Everything Numbers • ©The Mailbox® Books • TEC61111

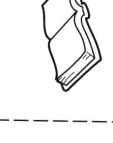

Name _____

Counting Nuts

Count.

Circle the set that has fewer.

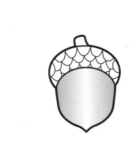

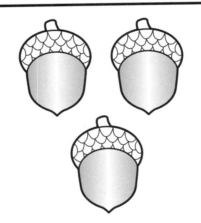

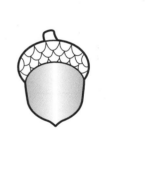

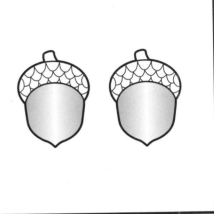

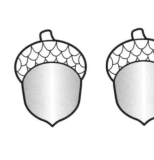

Ones Only

🖍 Color.

5	3	1	1	5	0
2	0	1	1	0	2
4	0	1	1	4	3
5	3	1	1	2	5
0	2	1	1	3	4

Everything Numbers • ©The Mailbox® Books • TEC61111

Note to the teacher: Have the child color each grid space that shows a numeral 1.

two

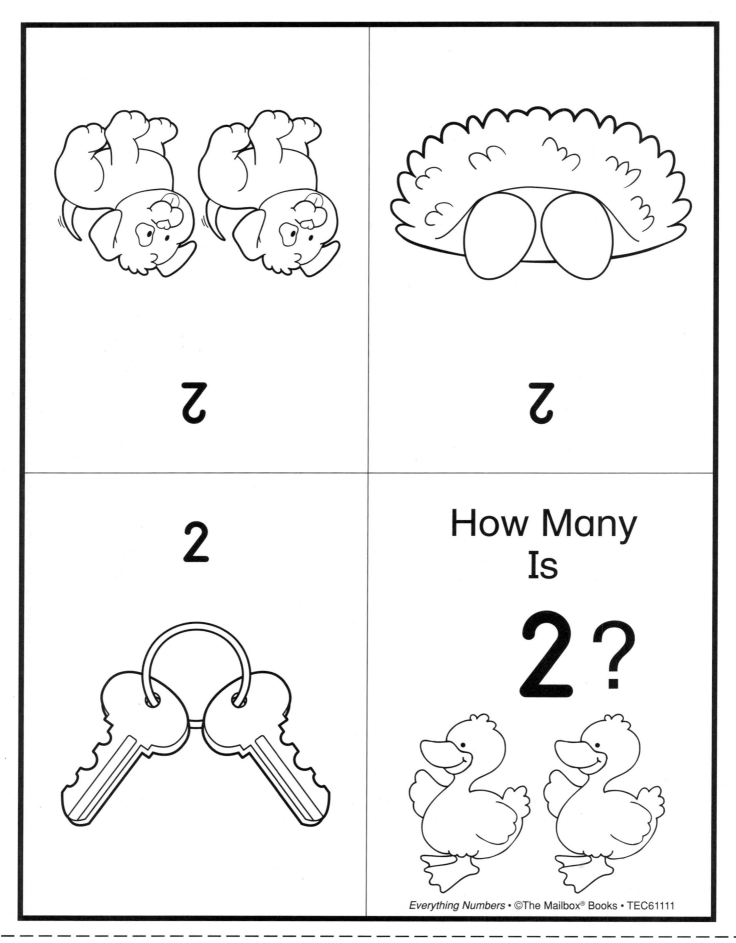

2

2

2

How Many
Is

2?

Everything Numbers • ©The Mailbox® Books • TEC61111

Fold-and-Go Booklet: To make a booklet, cut on the bold line. Fold along the thin horizontal line (keeping the programming to the outside) and then fold along the thin vertical line (keeping the cover to the outside).

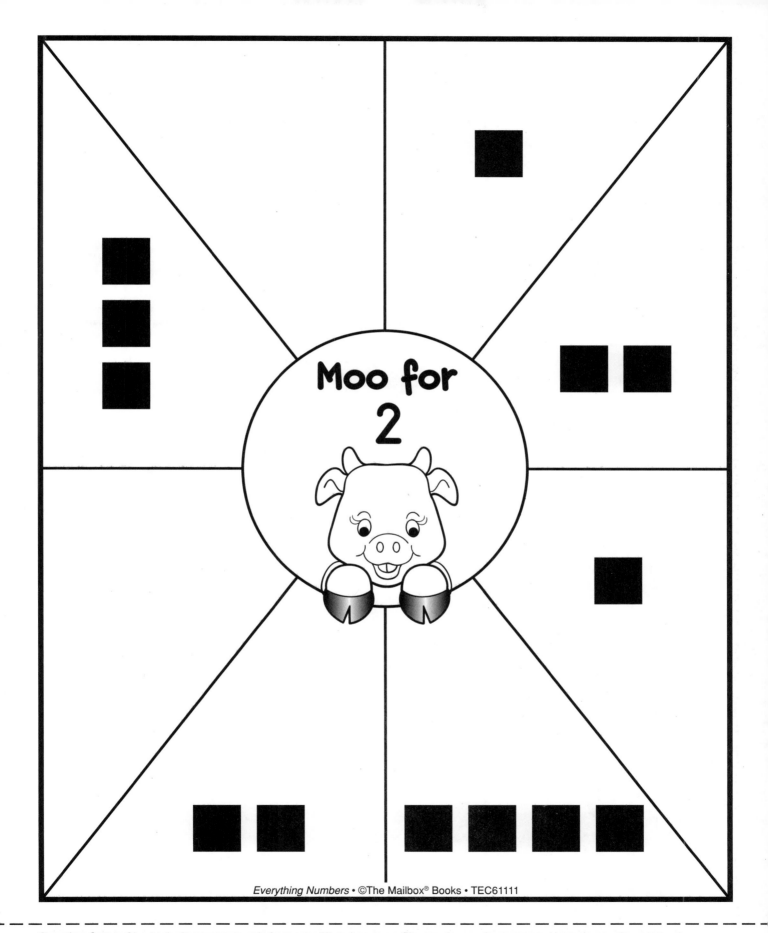

Moo for 2

Everything Numbers • ©The Mailbox® Books • TEC61111

Counting Game: Give each player a game strip from page 24 and a crayon. Players also need a pom-pom. Have players alternate tossing the pom-pom onto the gameboard. A player counts the squares in the game space where the pom-pom lands. When the pom-pom lands in the center circle or on a game space with two squares, the player says "two" and moos; then she traces a 2 on her game strip. Play continues until one player traces all her numbers or until game time is over.

23

Moo!

| 2 | 2 | 2 | 2 | 2 |

TEC61111

Moo!

| 2 | 2 | 2 | 2 | 2 |

TEC61111

Moo!

| 2 | 2 | 2 | 2 | 2 |

Everything Numbers • ©The Mailbox® Books • TEC61111

Two Lizards

Color each ⬡ that has 2.

 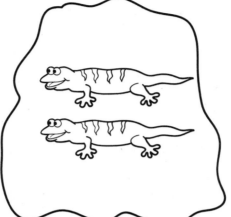 

 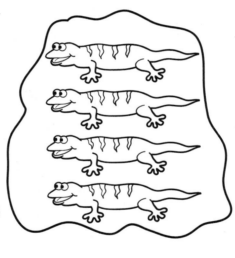 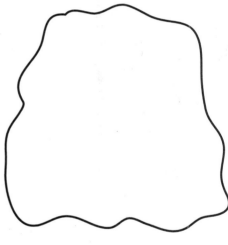

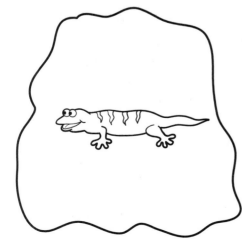  

Name _____

Number Two Train

Trace.

Cut.

Glue.

Everything Numbers • ©The Mailbox® Books • TEC61111

Note to the teacher: Have the child trace the numeral 2. Next, have her cut out the pictures and glue on the train each picture that shows two cookies.

Name_____

Counting Bananas

Count.

Circle the set that has more.

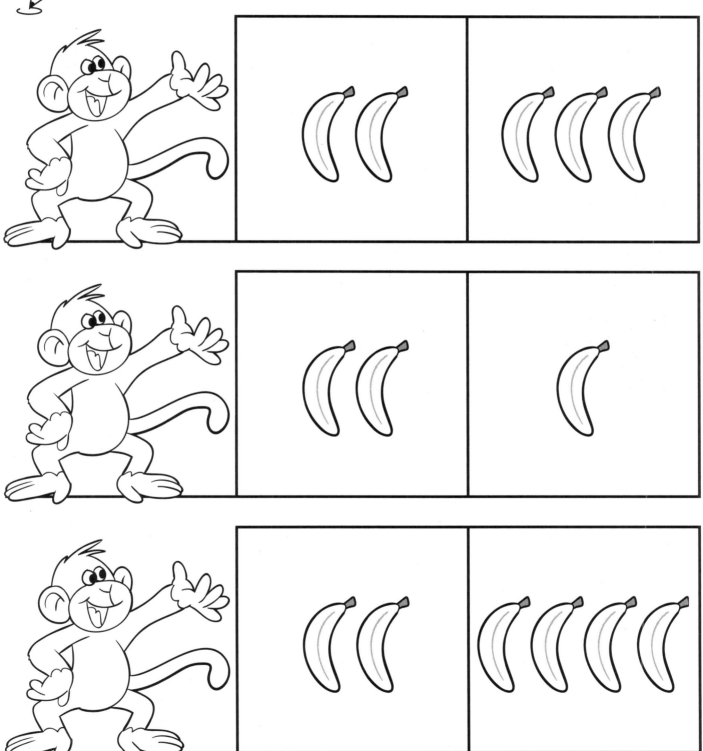

Name_____   Two: number recognition

Twos Only

🖍 Color.

4	2	2	2	2	5
1	3	0	6 2	2	4
3	0	5 2	2	2 6	3
4	1 2	2	2 0	5	4
5	2	2	2	2	4

Everything Numbers • ©The Mailbox® Books • TEC61111

28 **Note to the teacher:** Have the child color each grid space that shows a numeral 2.

three

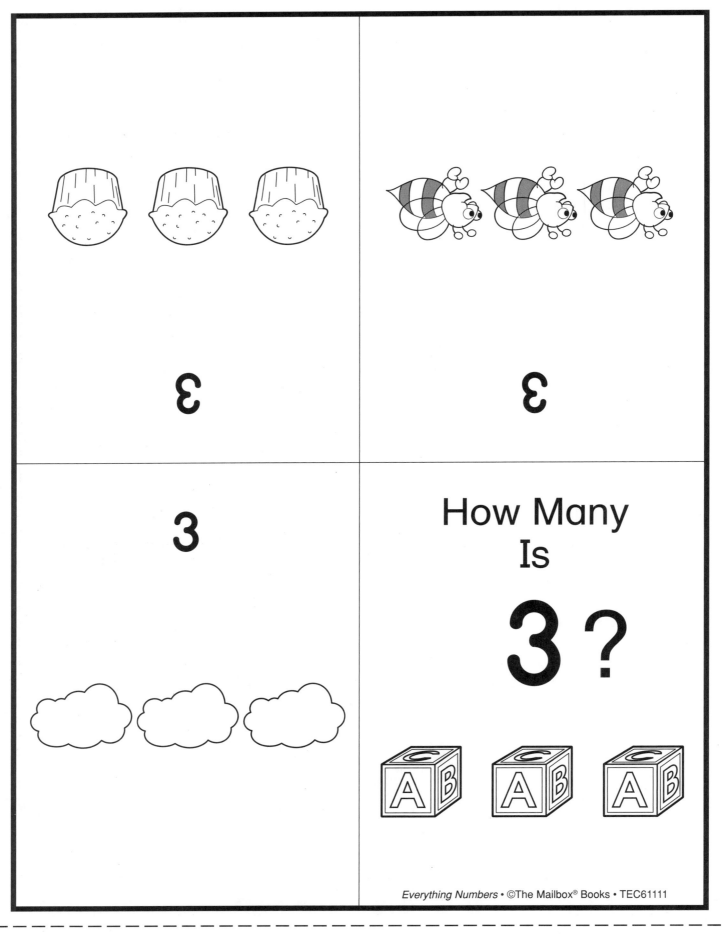

ε

ε

3

How Many
Is

3?

Fold-and-Go Booklet: To make a booklet, cut on the bold line. Fold along the thin horizontal line (keeping the programming to the outside) and then fold along the thin vertical line (keeping the cover to the outside).

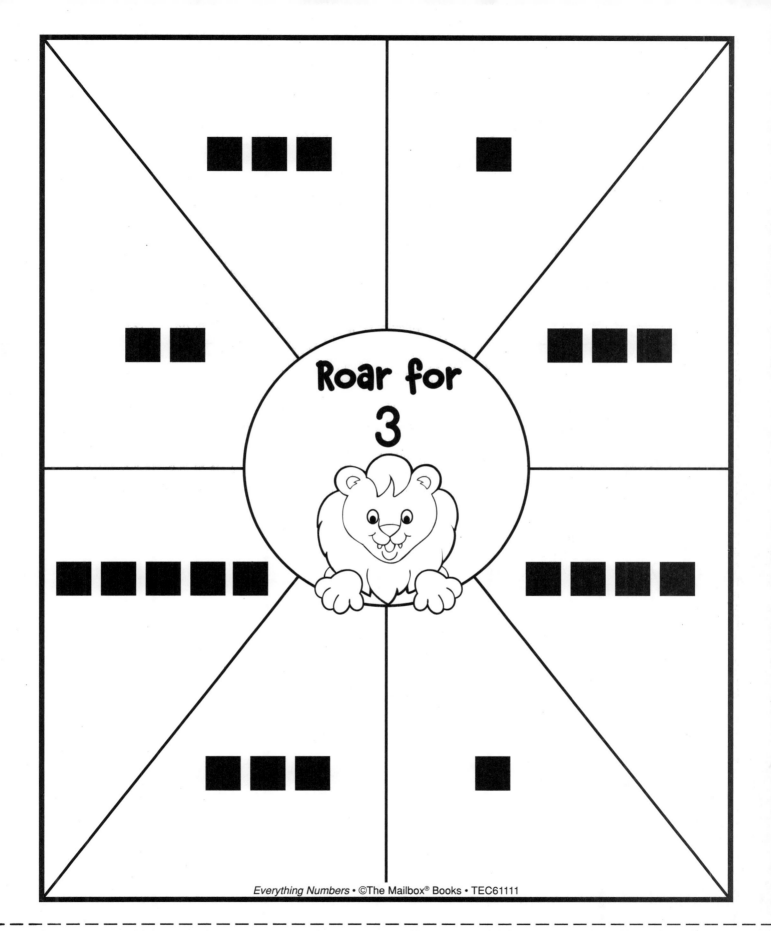

Counting Game: Give each player a game strip from page 32 and a crayon. Players also need a pom-pom. Have players alternate tossing the pom-pom onto the gameboard. A player counts the squares in the game space where the pom-pom lands. When the pom-pom lands in the center circle or on a game space with three squares, the player says "three" and roars; then he traces a 3 on his game strip. Play continues until one player traces all his numbers or until game time is over.

Roar!

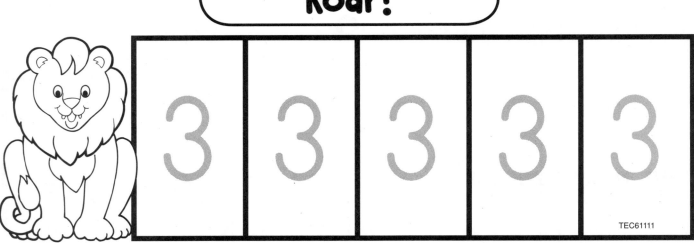

3 3 3 3 3

TEC61111

Roar!

3 3 3 3 3

TEC61111

Roar!

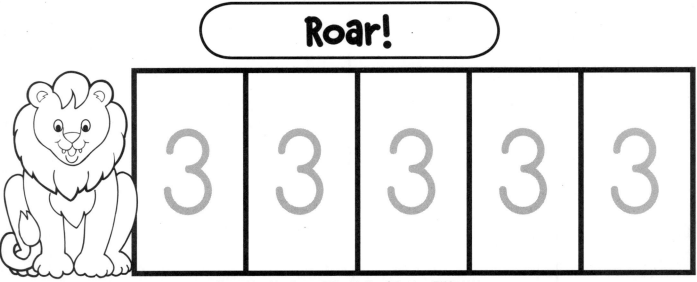

3 3 3 3 3

Everything Numbers • ©The Mailbox® Books • TEC61111

Name_____

Three Frogs

Color each  that has 3.

Name _____

Number Three Train

Trace.

Cut.

Glue.

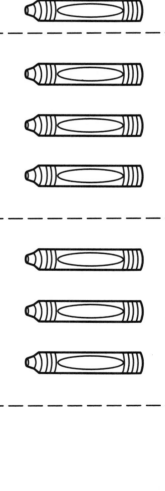

Everything Numbers • ©The Mailbox® Books • TEC61111

Note to the teacher: Have the child trace the numeral 3. Next, have him cut out the pictures and glue on the train each picture that shows three crayons.

34

Name _____

Counting Cheese

 Count.

Circle the set that has fewer.

Threes Only

Color.

4	3	3	3	3	5
1	0	2	5	3	4
2	6	4	3	3	5
0	2	6	5	3	2
1	3	3	3	3	4

Everything Numbers • ©The Mailbox® Books • TEC61111

Note to the teacher: Have the child color each grid space that shows a numeral 3.

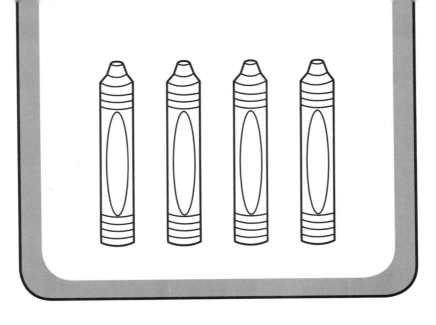

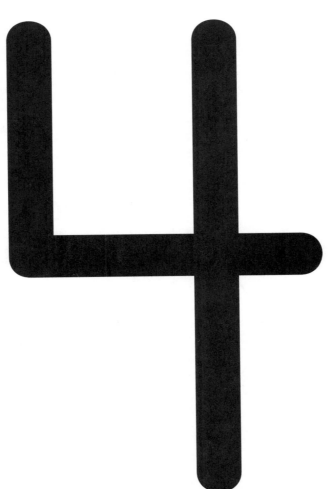

four

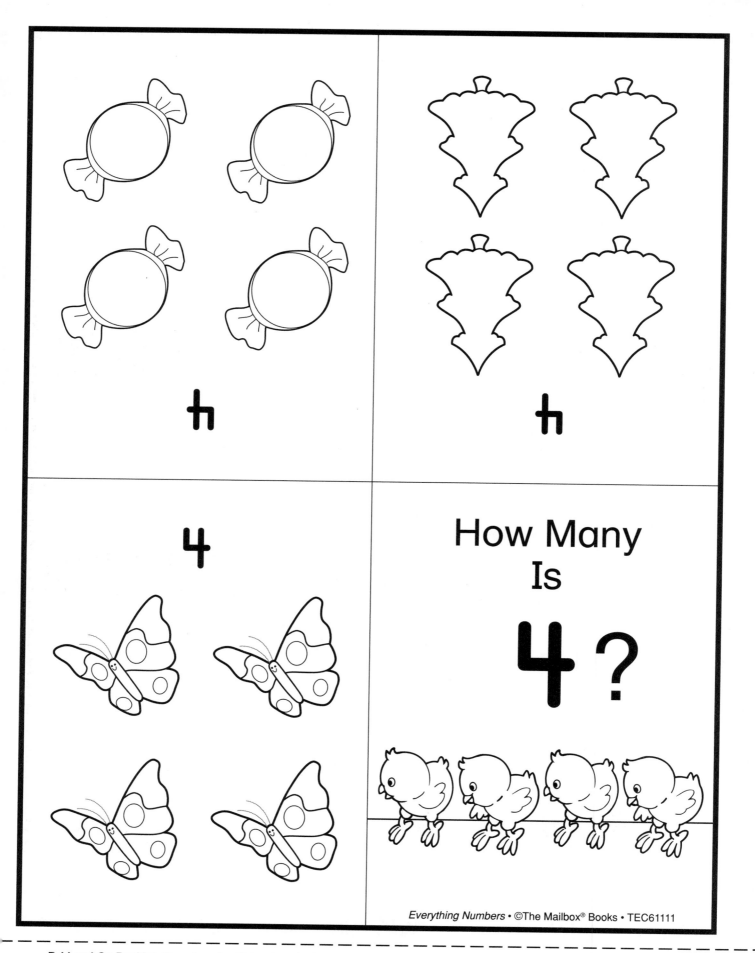

4

4

4

How Many Is 4?

Everything Numbers • ©The Mailbox® Books • TEC61111

Fold-and-Go Booklet: To make a booklet, cut on the bold line. Fold along the thin horizontal line (keeping the programming to the outside) and then fold along the thin vertical line (keeping the cover to the outside).

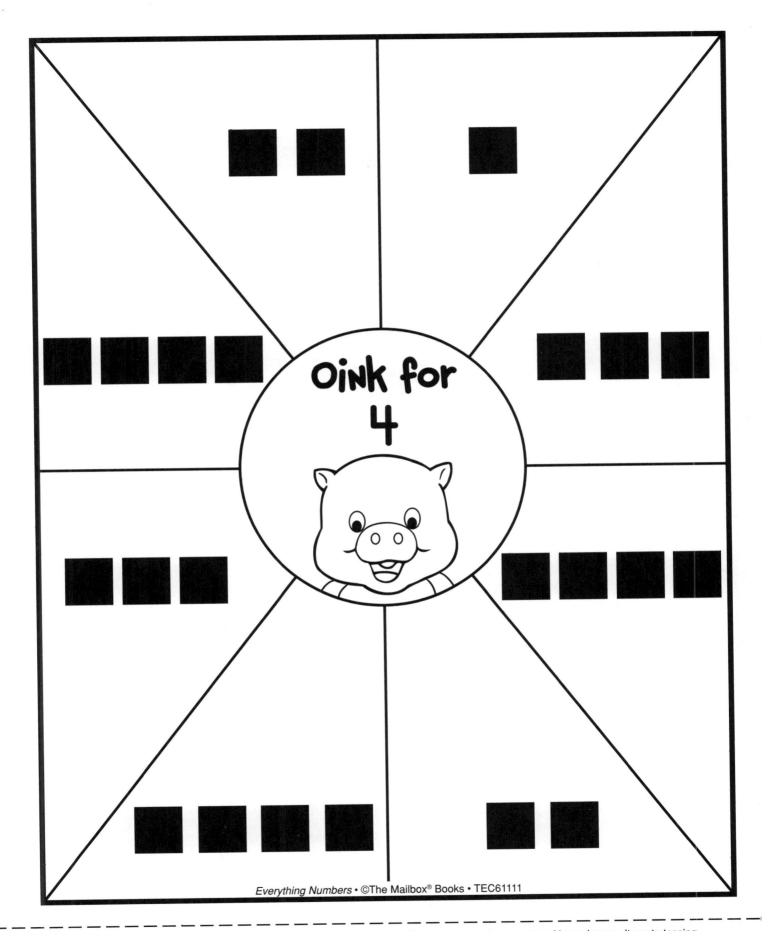

Everything Numbers • ©The Mailbox® Books • TEC61111

Counting Game: Give each player a game strip from page 40 and a crayon. Players also need a pom-pom. Have players alternate tossing the pom-pom onto the gameboard. A player counts the squares in the game space where the pom-pom lands. When the pom-pom lands in the center circle or on a game space with four squares, the player says "four" and oinks; then she traces a 4 on her game strip. Play continues until one player traces all her numbers or until game time is over.

Oink!

4 4 4 4 4

TEC61111

Oink!

4 4 4 4 4

TEC61111

Oink!

4 4 4 4 4

Everything Numbers • ©The Mailbox® Books • TEC61111

Game Strips: Use with "Oink for 4" on page 39.

Name _____

Four Flowers

 Color each that has 4.

Name _____

Number Four Train

Trace.

Cut.

Glue.

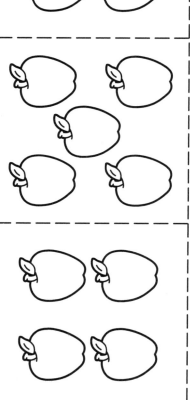

Everything Numbers • ©The Mailbox® Books • TEC61111

42

Note to the teacher: Have the child trace the numeral 4. Next, have her cut out the pictures and glue on the train each picture that shows four apples.

Name_____

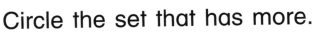

Counting Carrots

Count.

Circle the set that has more.

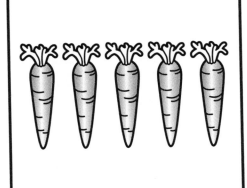

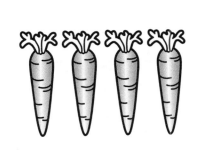

Fours Only

🖍 Color.

2	4	5	6	4	1
0	4	7	2	4	3
5	4	4	4	4	6
2	6	3	7	4	3
0	5	7	1	4	0

Everything Numbers • ©The Mailbox® Books • TEC61111

Note to the teacher: Have the child color each grid space that shows a numeral 4.

five

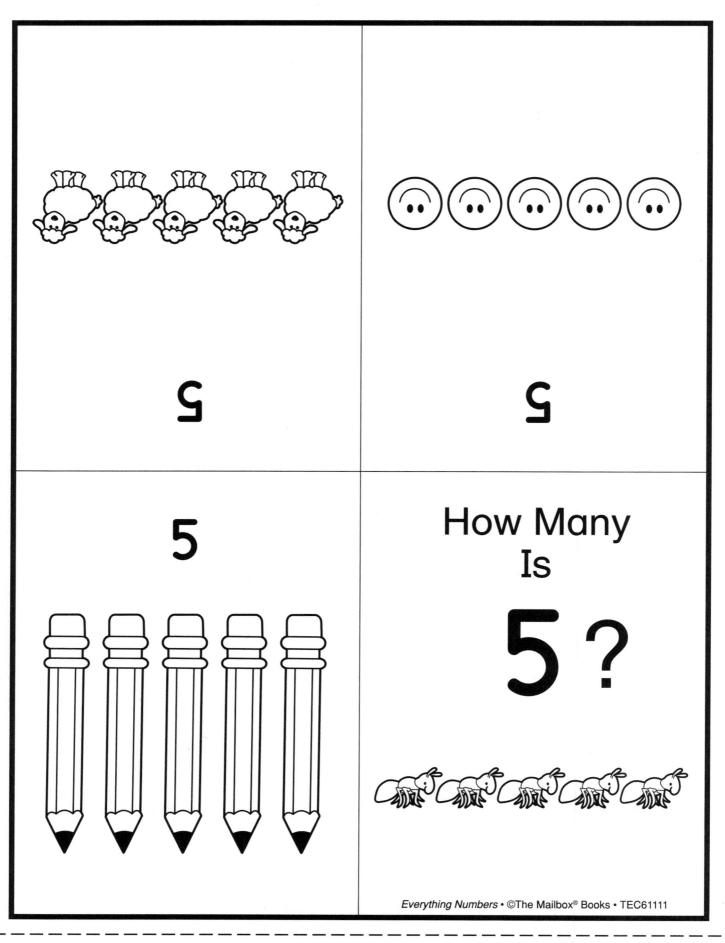

5

5

5

How Many Is

5?

Fold-and-Go Booklet: To make a booklet, cut on the bold line. Fold along the thin horizontal line (keeping the programming to the outside) and then fold along the thin vertical line (keeping the cover to the outside).

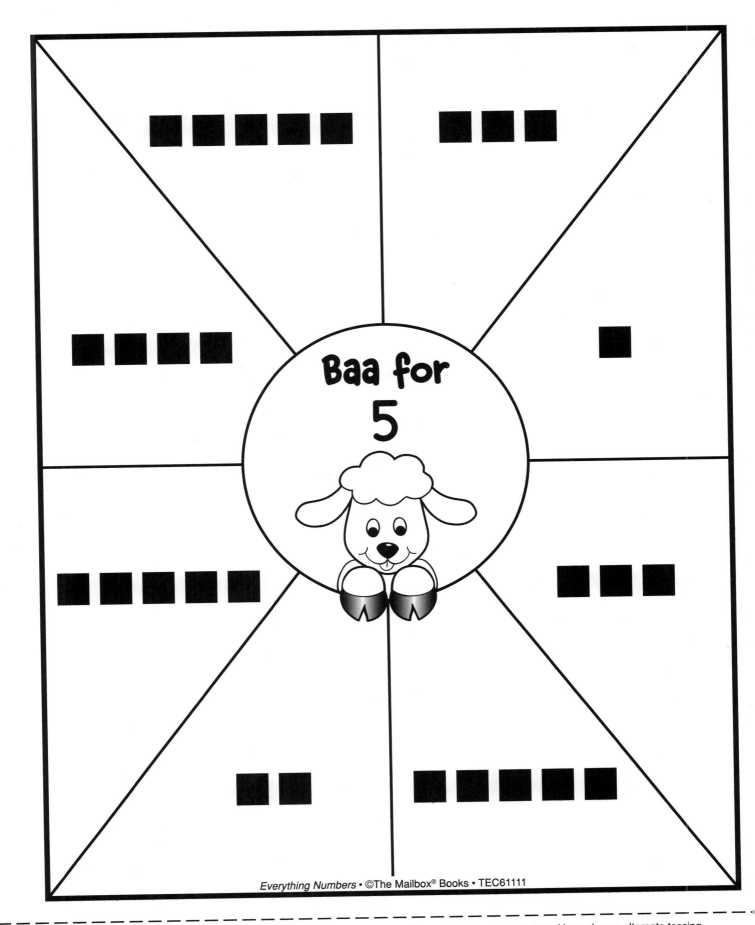

Baa for 5

Counting Game: Give each player a game strip from page 48 and a crayon. Players also need a pom-pom. Have players alternate tossing the pom-pom onto the gameboard. A player counts the squares in the game space where the pom-pom lands. When the pom-pom lands in the center circle or on a game space with five squares, the player says "five" and baas; then he traces a 5 on his game strip. Play continues until one player traces all his numbers or until game time is over.

Baa!

5	5	5	5	5

TEC61111

Baa!

5	5	5	5	5

TEC61111

Baa!

5	5	5	5	5

Everything Numbers • ©The Mailbox® Books • TEC61111

Name_____

highName_____ Name_____

Name_____

Name_____

Name_____

Five: number sets

Five Spots

Color each  that has 5.

Everything Numbers • ©The Mailbox® Books • TEC61111

49

Name _____

50

Five: number sets

Number Five Train

Trace.

Cut.

Glue.

Everything Numbers • ©The Mailbox® Books • TEC61111

Note to the teacher: Have the child trace the numeral 5. Next, have him cut out the pictures and glue on the train each picture that shows five footballs.

Counting Flies

Count.

Circle the set that has fewer.

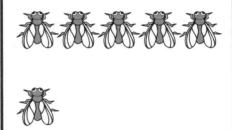

Fives Only

🖍 Color.

6	5	5	5	5	7
8	5	2	8	3	1
0	5	5	5	5	7
6	4	2	1	5	8
0	5	5	5	5	6

52   **Note to the teacher:** Have the child color each grid space that shows a numeral 5.

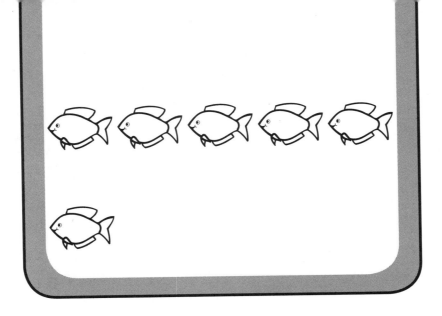

six

9

9

6

How Many
Is

6?

Everything Numbers • ©The Mailbox® Books • TEC61111

Fold-and-Go Booklet: To make a booklet, cut on the bold line. Fold along the thin horizontal line (keeping the programming to the outside) and then fold along the thin vertical line (keeping the cover to the outside).

Counting Game: Give each player a game strip from page 56 and a crayon. Players also need a pom-pom. Have players alternate tossing the pom-pom onto the gameboard. A player counts the squares in the game space where the pom-pom lands. When the pom-pom lands in the center circle or on a game space with six squares, the player says "six" and barks; then she traces a 6 on her game strip. Play continues until one player traces all her numbers or until game time is over.

Bark!

Bark!

Bark!

Everything Numbers • ©The Mailbox® Books • TEC61111

Game Strips: Use with "Bark for 6" on page 55.

Six Gumballs

Color 6 ◯ in each .

Name _____

Number Six Train

Trace.

Cut.

Glue.

6

Everything Numbers • ©The Mailbox® Books • TEC61111

Note to the teacher: Have the child trace the numeral 6. Next, have her cut out the pictures and glue on the train the picture that shows six pieces of candy.

Name<u>   </u>

Counting Ducklings

 Count.

 Circle the set that has more.

Name_____

Six: number recognition

Sixes Only

🖍 Color.

6

1	3	5	6	6	8
6					
8	5	6	6	2	1
			4		
7	5	6	6	6	2
3	7	6	2	6	3
1	0	6	6	6	4

Everything Numbers • ©The Mailbox® Books • TEC61111

60   **Note to the teacher:** Have the child color each grid space that shows a numeral 6.

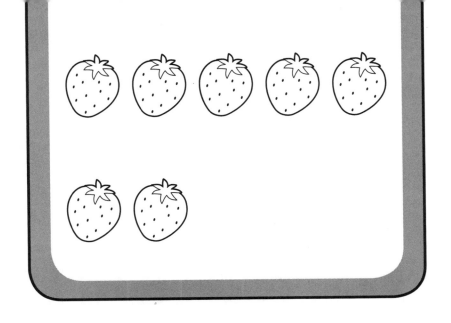

seven

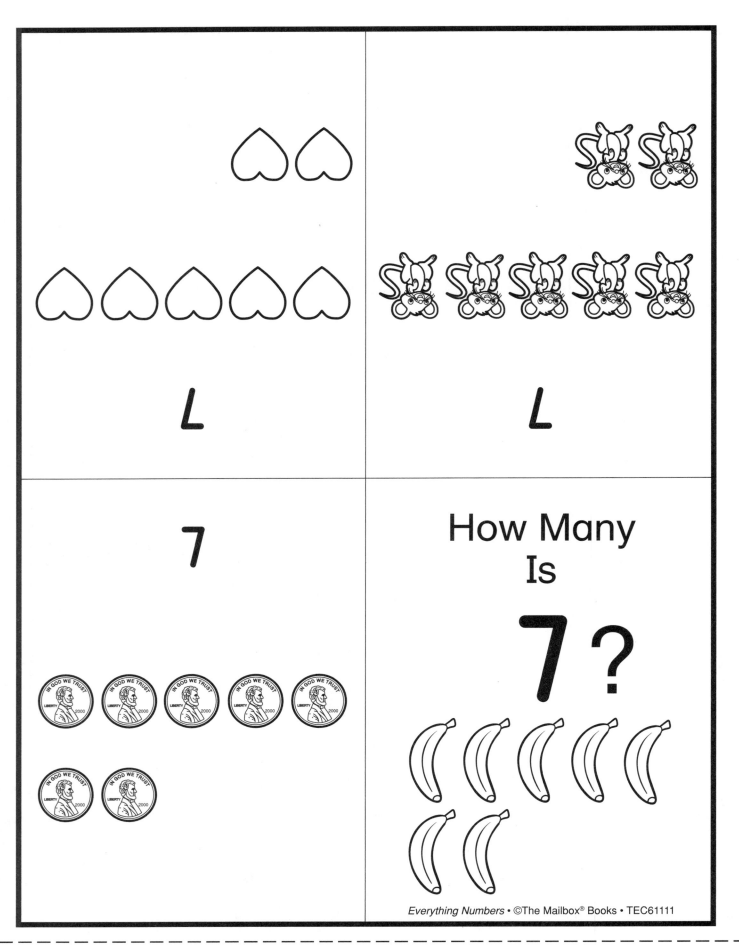

𝐿

𝐿

7

How Many
Is

7?

Fold-and-Go Booklet: To make a booklet, cut on the bold line. Fold along the thin horizontal line (keeping the programming to the outside) and then fold along the thin vertical line (keeping the cover to the outside).

Counting Game: Give each player a game strip from page 64 and a crayon. Players also need a pom-pom. Have players alternate tossing the pom-pom onto the gameboard. A player counts the squares in the game space where the pom-pom lands. When the pom-pom lands in the center circle or on a game space with seven squares, the player says "seven" and squeaks; then he traces a 7 on his game strip. Play continues until one player traces all his numbers or until game time is over.

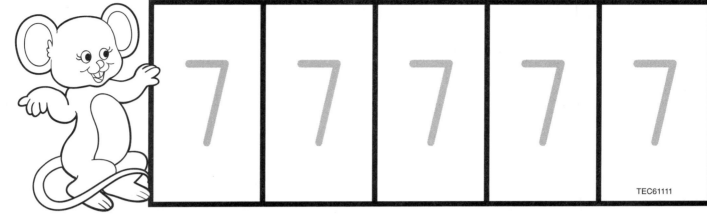

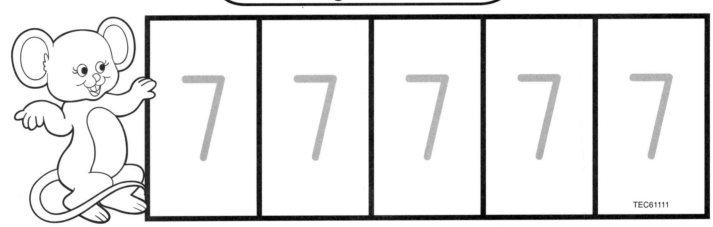

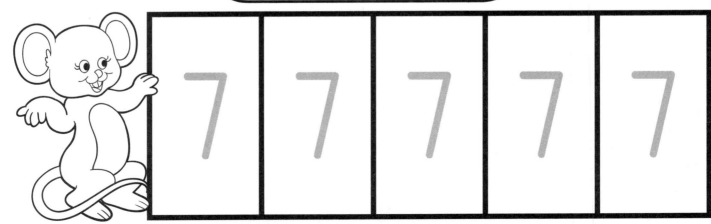

Everything Numbers • ©The Mailbox® Books • TEC61111

Seven Birds

 Color 7  in each  .

Name —————

Number Seven Train

Trace.

Cut.

Glue.

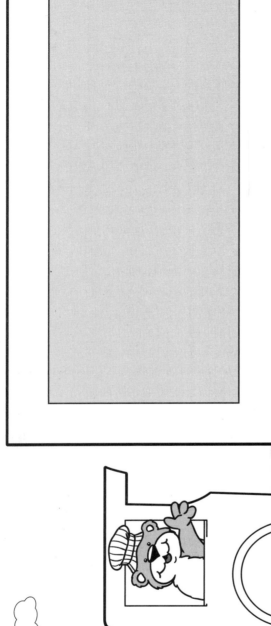

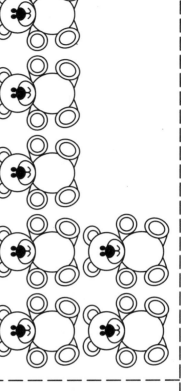

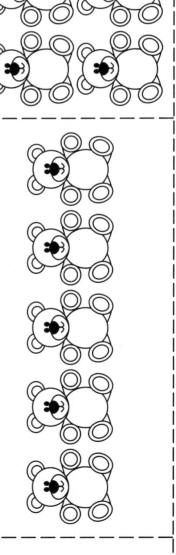

Everything Numbers • ©The Mailbox® Books • TEC61111

Note to the teacher: Have the child trace the numeral 7. Next, have him cut out the pictures and glue on the train the picture that shows seven teddy bears.

Name_____

Counting Presents

Count.

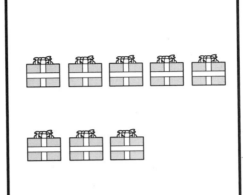 Circle the set that has fewer.

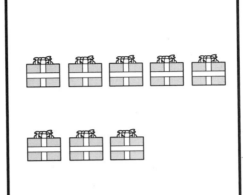

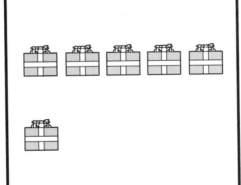
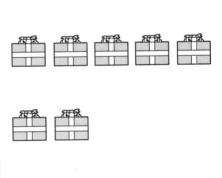

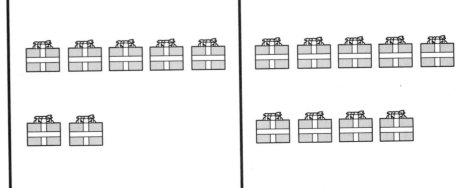
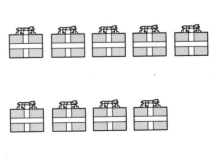

Sevens Only

🖍 Color.

8	7	7	7	7	3
4	5	2	1	7	0
9	10	4	7	3	10
0	1	7	4	2	5
6	7	2	4	3	6

Note to the teacher: Have the child color each grid space that shows a numeral 7.

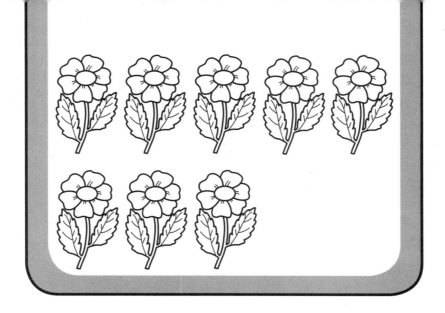

eight

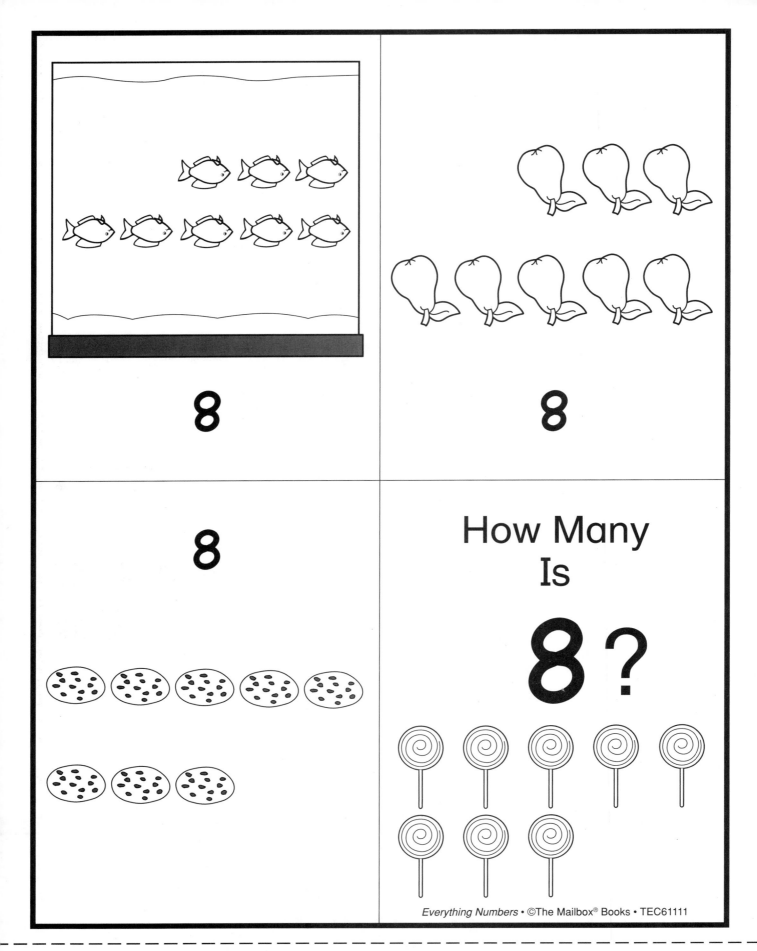

8

8

8

How Many
Is

8?

Everything Numbers • ©The Mailbox® Books • TEC61111

Fold-and-Go Booklet: To make a booklet, cut on the bold line. Fold along the thin horizontal line (keeping the programming to the outside) and then fold along the thin vertical line (keeping the cover to the outside).

Counting Game: Give each player a game strip from page 72 and a crayon. Players also need a pom-pom. Have players alternate tossing the pom-pom onto the gameboard. A player counts the squares in the game space where the pom-pom lands. When the pom-pom lands in the center circle or on a game space with eight squares, the player says "eight" and tweets; then she traces an 8 on her game strip. Play continues until one player traces all her numbers or until game time is over.

Everything Numbers • ©The Mailbox® Books • TEC61111

Tweet!

8	8	8	8	8

TEC61111

Tweet!

8	8	8	8	8

TEC61111

Tweet!

8	8	8	8	8

Everything Numbers • ©The Mailbox® Books • TEC61111

Eight Scoops

 Color 8 🍨 on each 🥣.

Name _____

Number Eight Train

Trace.

Cut.

Glue.

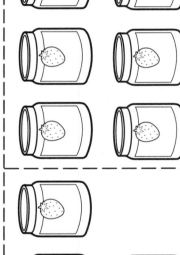

Everything Numbers • ©The Mailbox® Books • TEC61111

Note to the teacher: Have the child trace the numeral 8. Next, have her cut out the pictures and glue on the train the picture that shows eight jars.

74

Counting Books

Count.

Circle the set that has more.

Name_____

Eights Only

🖍 Color.

8

6	8	8	8	8	10
4	8	8	2	8	8	1
2		8	8		5
6	8	8	3	8	8	3
9	8	8	8	8	10

Note to the teacher: Have the child color each grid space that shows a numeral 8.

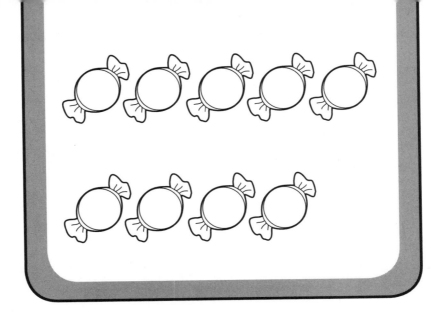

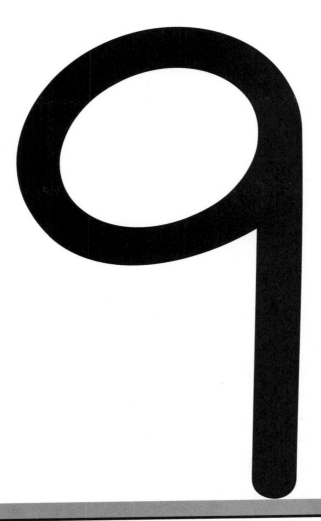

nine

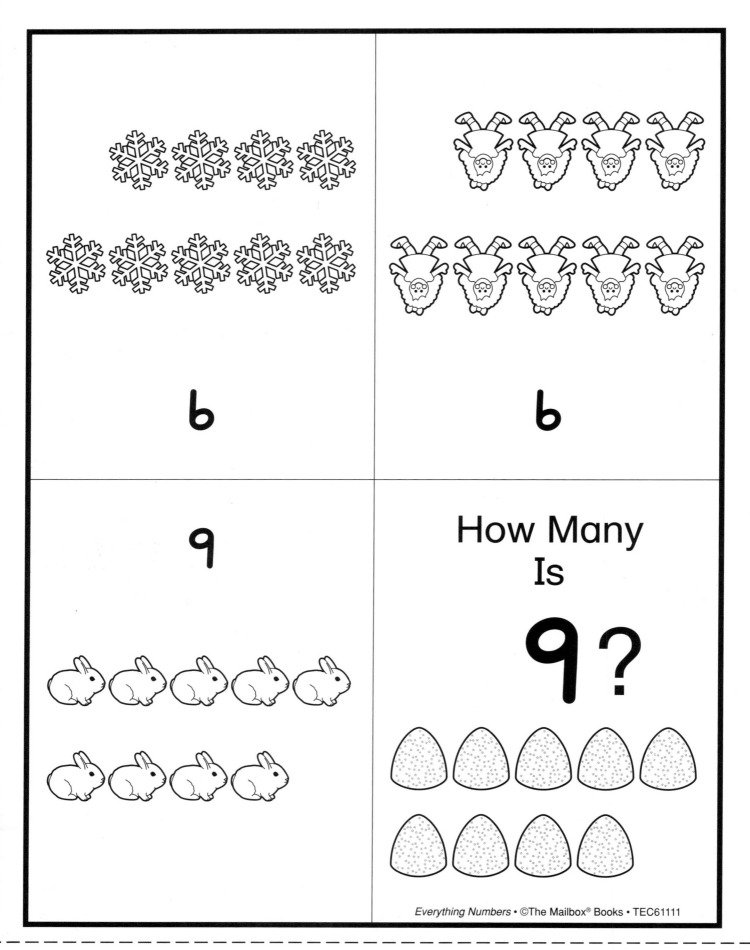

6

6

9

How Many
Is

9?

Fold-and-Go Booklet: To make a booklet, cut on the bold line. Fold along the thin horizontal line (keeping the programming to the outside) and then fold along the thin vertical line (keeping the cover to the outside).

Counting Game: Give each player a game strip from page 80 and a crayon. Players also need a pom-pom. Have players alternate tossing the pom-pom onto the gameboard. A player counts the squares in the game space where the pom-pom lands. When the pom-pom lands in the center circle or on a game space with nine squares, the player says "nine" and neighs; then he traces a 9 on his game strip. Play continues until one player traces all his numbers or until game time is over.

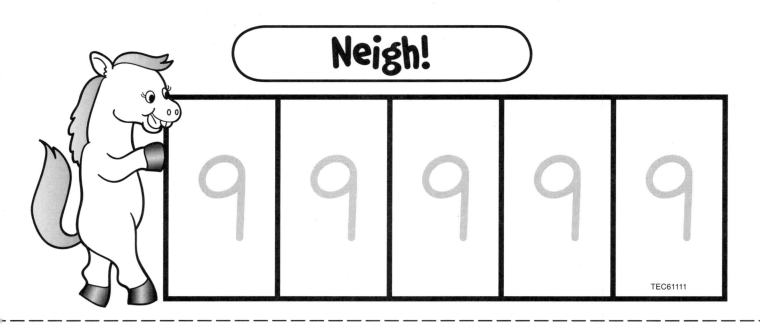

Neigh!

9 9 9 9 9

TEC61111

Neigh!

9 9 9 9 9

TEC61111

Neigh!

9 9 9 9 9

Everything Numbers • ©The Mailbox® Books • TEC61111

Game Strips: Use with "Neigh for 9" on page 79.

Nine Spots

Color 9 ◯ on each .

Name _____

Number Nine Train

Trace.

Cut.

Glue.

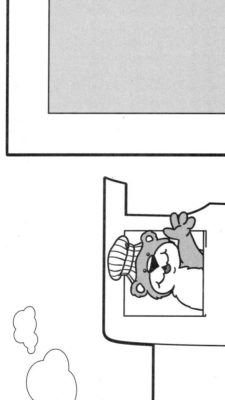

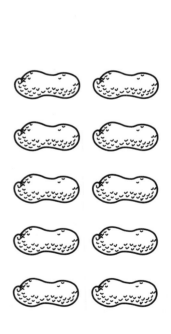

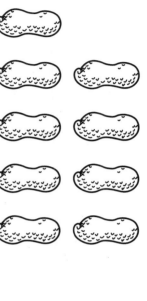

Everything Numbers • ©The Mailbox® Books • TEC61111

Note to the teacher: Have the child trace the numeral 9. Next, have him cut out the pictures and glue on the train the picture that shows nine peanuts.

Name _____

Counting Bones

Count.

 Circle the set that has fewer.

Nines Only

🖍 Color.

4	5	9	9	9	8
6	3	9	2	9	1
0	8	9	9	9	7
6	2	4	5	9	3
8	10	7	3	9	10

Note to the teacher: Have the child color each grid space that shows a numeral 9.

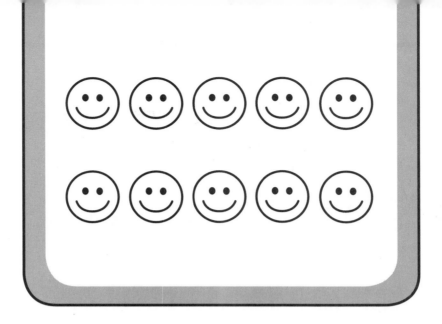

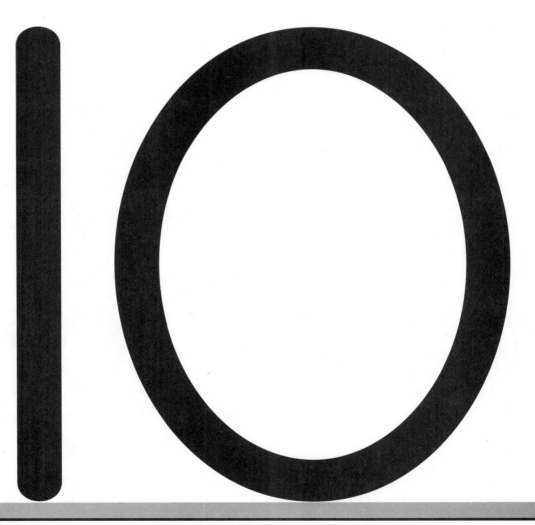

ten

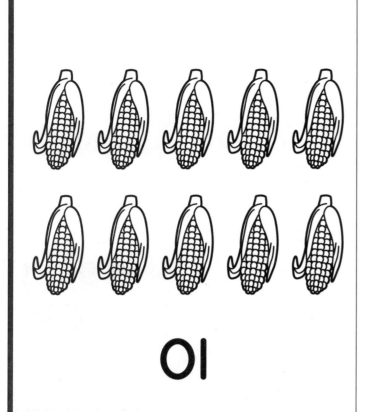

OI

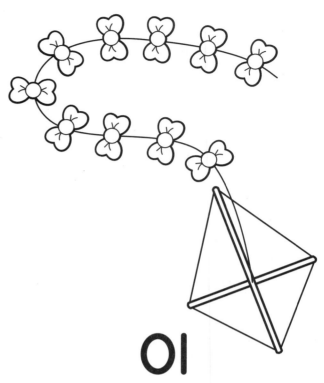

OI

IO

How Many
Is

10?

Everything Numbers • ©The Mailbox® Books • TEC61111

Fold-and-Go Booklet: To make a booklet, cut on the bold line. Fold along the thin horizontal line (keeping the programming to the outside) and then fold along the thin vertical line (keeping the cover to the outside).

Everything Numbers • ©The Mailbox® Books • TEC61111

Counting Game: Give each player a game strip from page 88 and a crayon. Players also need a pom-pom. Have players alternate tossing the pom-pom onto the gameboard. A player counts the squares in the game space where the pom-pom lands. When the pom-pom lands in the center circle or on a game space with ten squares, the player says "ten" and clucks; then she traces a 10 on her game strip. Play continues until one player traces all her numbers or until game time is over.

87

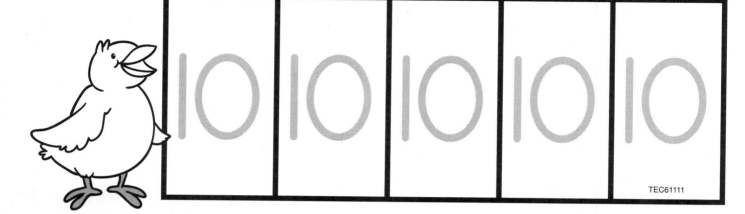

Cluck!

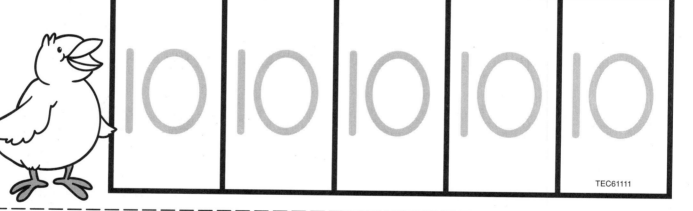

Cluck!

Cluck!

Everything Numbers • ©The Mailbox® Books • TEC61111

Ten Apples

Color 10 🍎 on each 🌳.

Name _____

Number Ten Train

Trace.

Cut.

Glue.

Everything Numbers • ©The Mailbox® Books • TEC61111

Note to the teacher: Have the child trace the numeral 10. Next, have her cut out the pictures and glue on the train the picture that shows ten carrots.

Name _____

Counting Toys

Count.

Circle the set that has more.

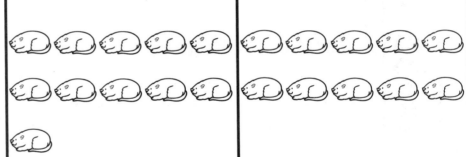

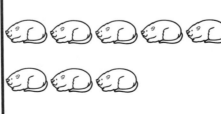

Name_____

TeNs ONly

Color.

10

10	4	10	10	10	4
10	6	10	3	10	8
10	3	10	7	10	7
10	8	10	1	10	6
10	9	10	10	10	5

Everything Numbers • ©The Mailbox® Books • TEC61111

Note to the teacher: Have the child color each grid space that shows a numeral 10.

eleven

11 Starfish

Finish the picture.

Note to the teacher: Read the title and have the child point to the starfish on the page. Have the child draw more starfish to total 11.

Name_____

 Count.

IN the GardeN

✏ Draw a line to the matching number.

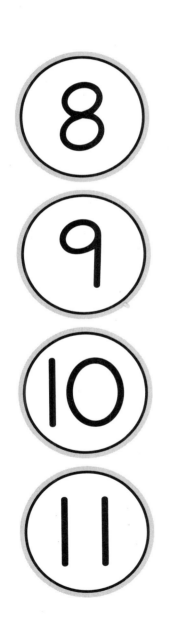

Find the Pond

Connect the dots in order from 0 to 11.

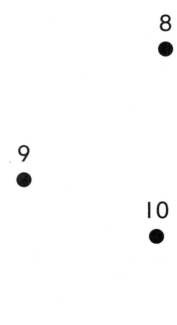

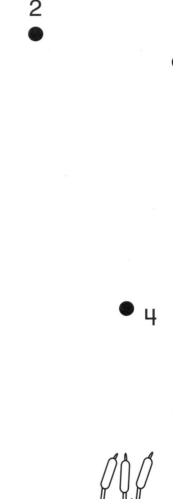

★
0

2

1

3

6

7

4

5

8

9

10

11

Everything Numbers • ©The Mailbox® Books • TEC61111

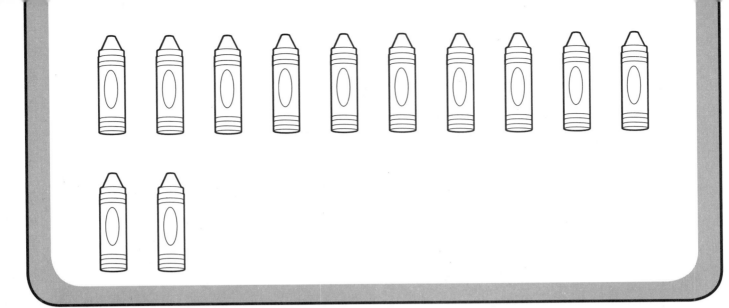

twelve

12 Cookies

Finish the picture.

Note to the teacher: Read the title and have the child point to the cookie on the page. Have the child draw more cookies to total 12.

Name_____

  Count.

 At School

Draw a line to the matching number.

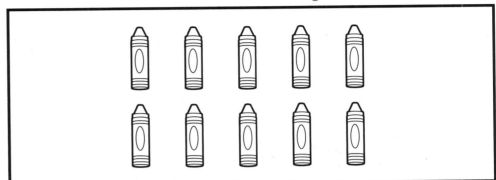

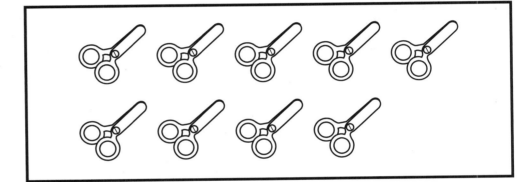

9

10

11

12

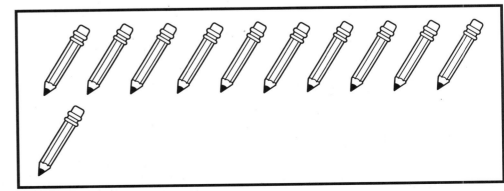

Find the Veggies

Connect the dots in order from 0 to 12.

0 ★

1

2

3

4

5

6

7

8

9

10

11

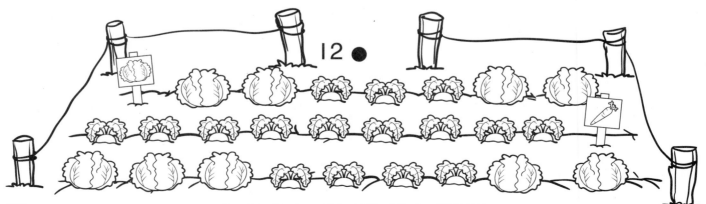

12

13

thirteen

13 Gumballs

Finish the picture.

Name_____

Count.

Draw a line to the matching number.

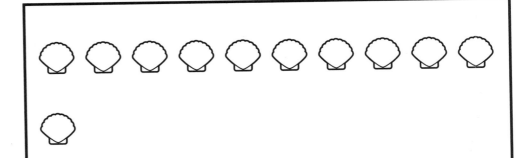

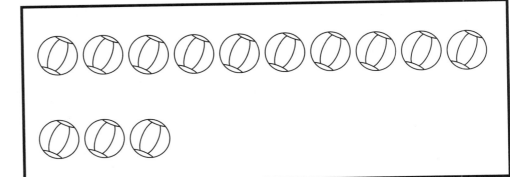

Find the Flowers

Connect the dots in order from 0 to 13.

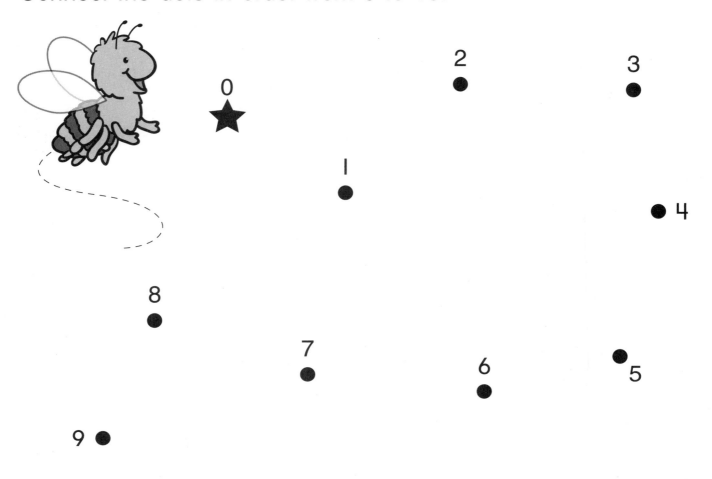

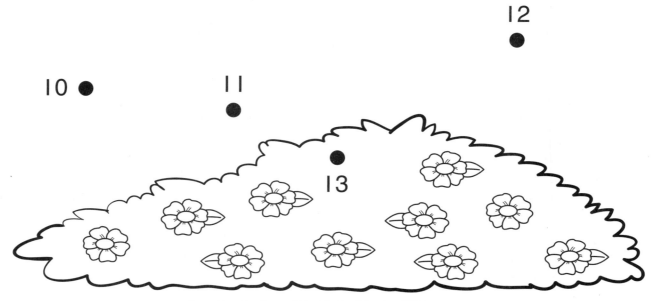

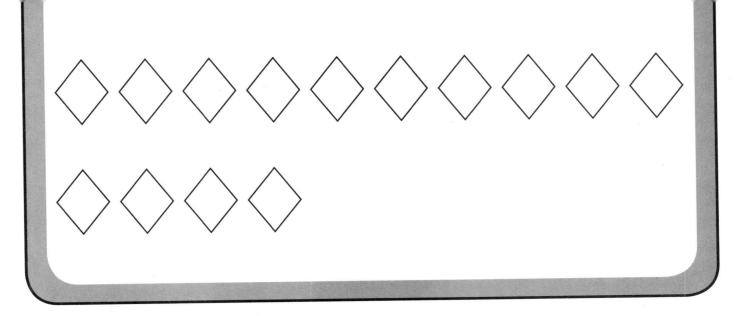

fourteen

14 Balloons

Finish the picture.

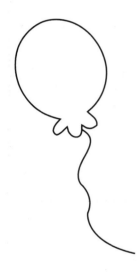

Note to the teacher: Read the title and have the child point to the balloon on the page. Have the child draw more balloons to total 14.

Name_____

 Count.

At the Circus

Draw a line to the matching number.

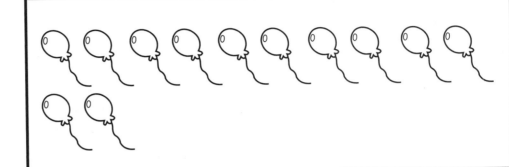

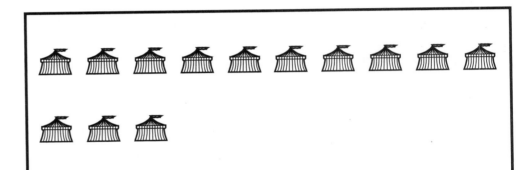

Name _____

Find Farmer Brown

Connect the dots in order from 0 to 14.

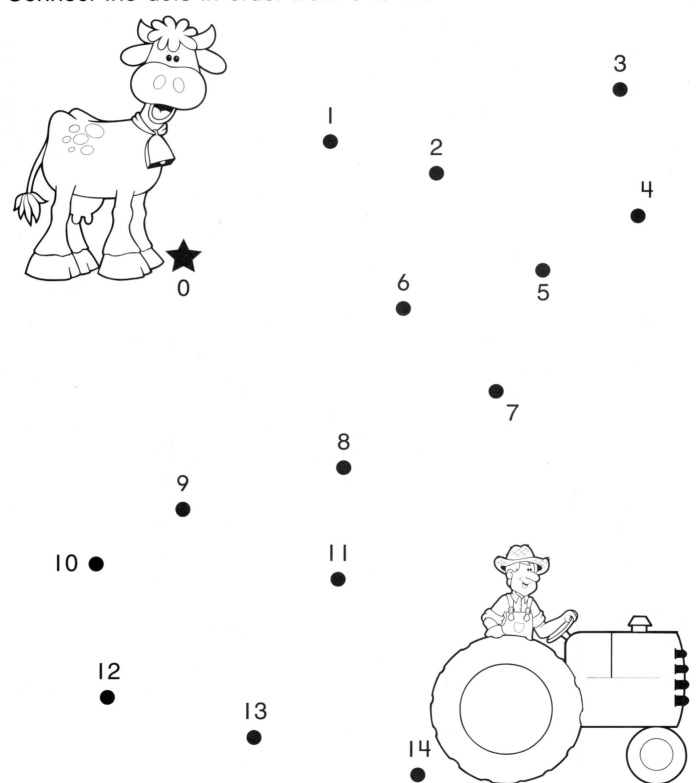

Everything Numbers • ©The Mailbox® Books • TEC61111

15

fifteen

15 Flowers

Finish the picture.

Note to the teacher: Read the title and have the child point to the flower on the page. Have the child draw more flowers to total 15.

Name_____

 Count.

Draw a line to the matching number.

At the Farm

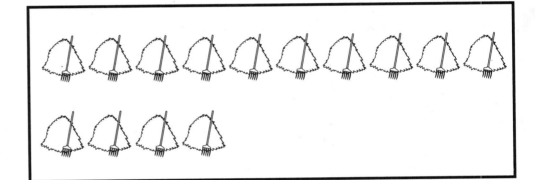

Name_____

Find the Cheese

Connect the dots in order from 0 to 15.

2

1

3

4

0

5

9

6

10

8

7

11

13

15

12

14

Everything Numbers • ©The Mailbox® Books • TEC61111

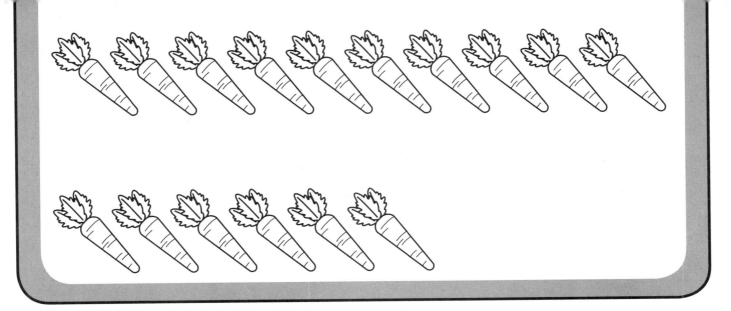

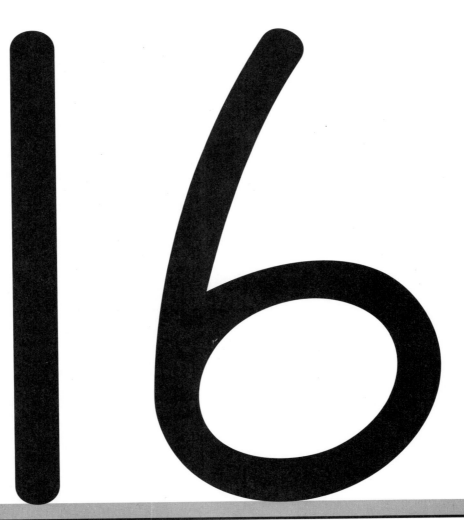

sixteen

16 Eggs

Finish the picture.

Note to the teacher: Read the title and have the child point to the egg on the page. Have the child draw more eggs to total 16.

Count.

Draw a line to the matching number.

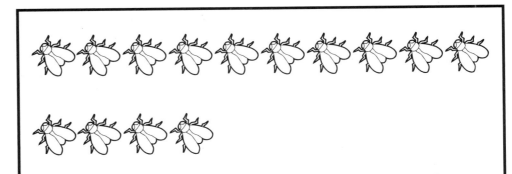 **At the Pond**

 13

 14

 15

 16

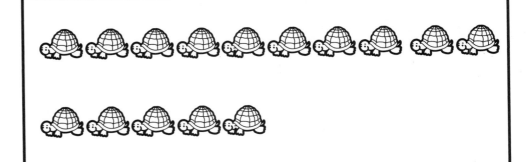

Find the Picnic

Connect the dots in order from 0 to 16.

0 ★

1 ●

2 ●

3 ●

4 ●

5 ●

11 ●

6 ●

7 ●

10 ●

12 ●

9 ●

13 ●

14 ●

8 ●

15 ●

16 ●

seventeen

17 Raindrops

Finish the picture.

Note to the teacher: Read the title and have the child point to the raindrop on the page. Have the child draw more raindrops to total 17.

Name _____

Count.

Draw a line to the matching number.

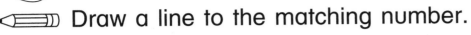

In the Forest

14

15

16

17

Find the Fly

Connect the dots in order from 0 to 17.

0 ★

1 ●

3 ●

2 ●

4 ●

5 ●

6 ●

7 ●

8 ●

9 ●

10 ●

11 ●

12 ●

13 ●

15 ●

14 ●

16 ●

17 ●

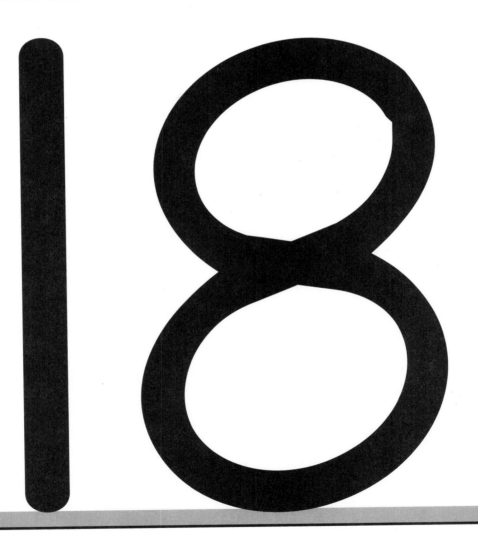

eighteen

Name _____

18 Lily Pads

Finish the picture.

Note to the teacher: Read the title and have the child point to the lily pad on the page. Have the child draw lily pads to total 18.

Name

 Count.

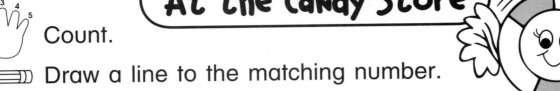

Draw a line to the matching number.

15

16

17

18

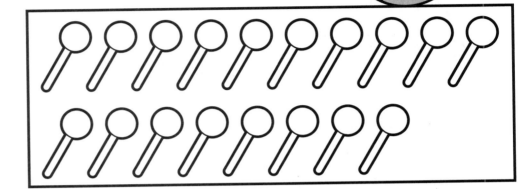

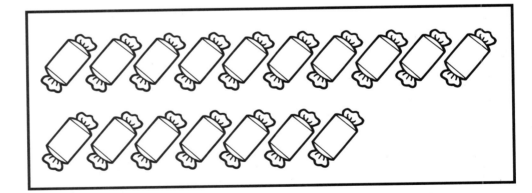

Name_____

Find the Zoo

Connect the dots in order from 0 to 18.

1

2

3

4

0 ★

6

7

5

8

9

12

13

11

10

14

15

16

ZOO

17

18

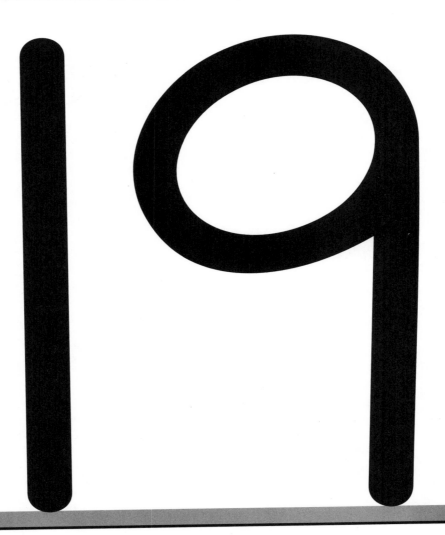

nineteen

19 Bones

Finish the picture.

Note to the teacher: Read the title and have the child point to the bone on the page. Have the child draw bones to total 19.

Name_____

At the Fair

 Count.

Draw a line to the matching number.

16

17

18

19

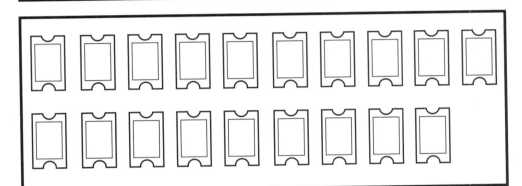

Find the Honey

Connect the dots in order from 0 to 19.

3
2
1
4
0 ⭐
6
5
8 7
9
11 12
10 13
15
14
16
18 19
17

Everything Numbers • ©The Mailbox® Books • TEC61111

20
twenty

20 Apples

Finish the picture.

Note to the teacher: Read the title and have the child point to the apple on the page. Have the child draw more apples to total 20.

Name_____

At the Toy Store

 Count.

Draw a line to the matching number.

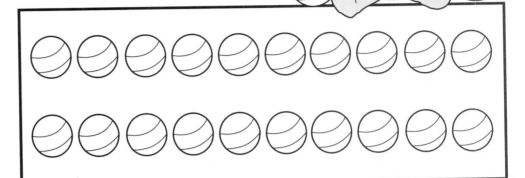

Find the Nest

Connect the dots in order from 0 to 20.

0 ★

1 ●

2 ●

3 ●

4 ●

5 ●

6 ●

7 ●

8 ●

9 ●

10 ●

11 ●

12 ●

13 ●

14 ●

15 ●

16 ●

17 ●

18 ●

19 ●

20 ●

Everything Numbers • ©The Mailbox® Books • TEC61111

Preparing and using the cards:

Make one construction paper copy of the cards. Cut out the cards and use them as desired. Possible activities include

- counting practice
- number identification practice
- number recognition practice
- number word recognition
- number and number set matching
- number and number word matching

Make two construction paper copies of the cards. Cut out the cards and use them to play a variety of memory games.

zero

TEC61111

TEC61111

O

TEC61111

Number Cards
Use with the directions on page 133.

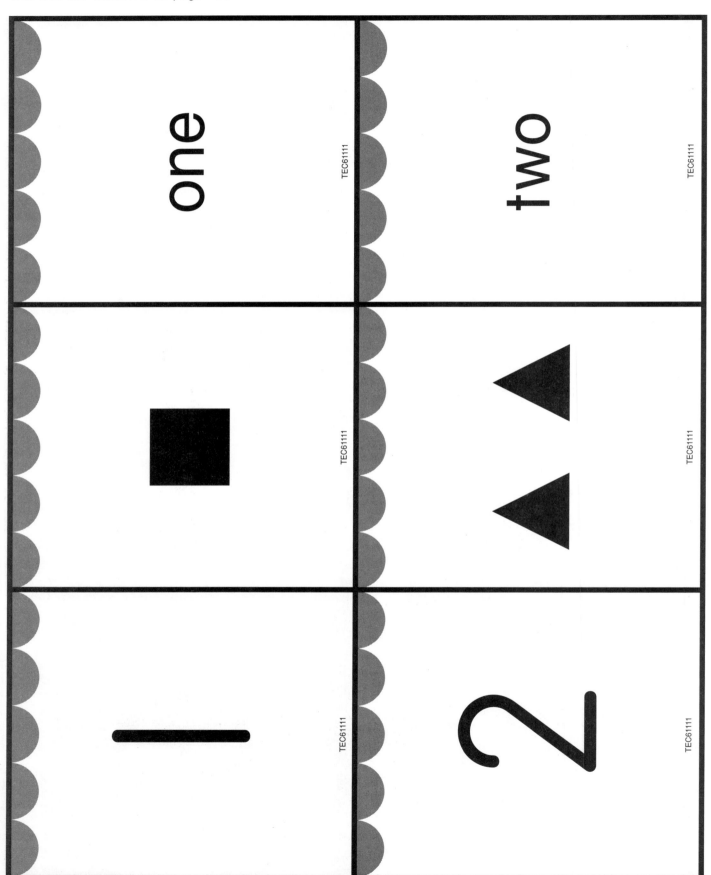

one

TEC61111

two

TEC61111

TEC61111

TEC61111

TEC61111

2

TEC61111

Everything Numbers • ©The Mailbox® Books • TEC61111

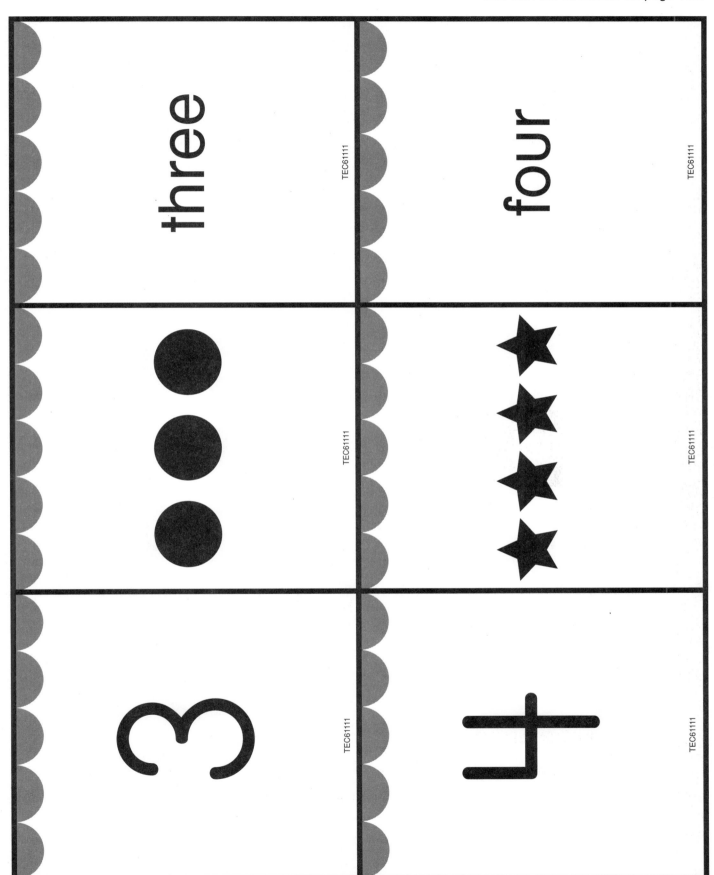

three

TEC61111

four

TEC61111

TEC61111

TEC61111

3

TEC61111

4

TEC61111

Number Cards

Use with the directions on page 133.

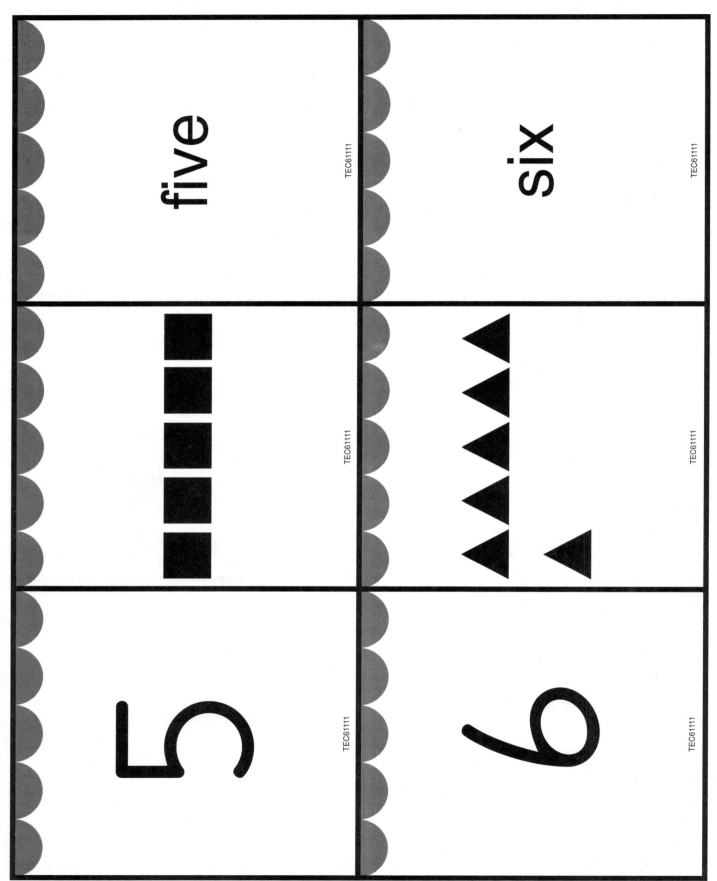

five

six

5

6

TEC61111

Everything Numbers • ©The Mailbox® Books • TEC61111

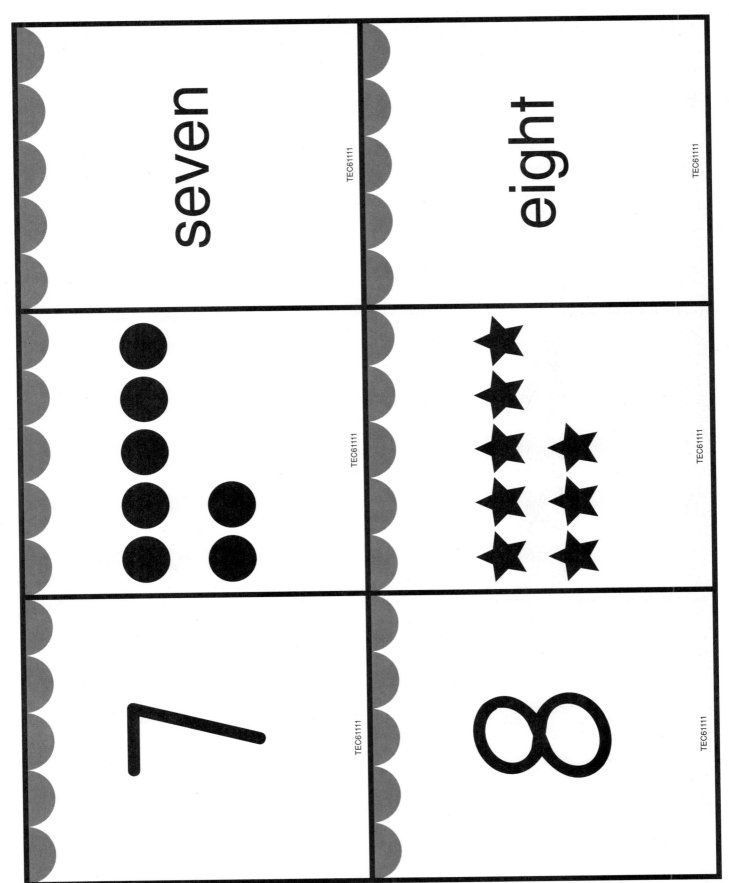

seven

TEC61111

eight

TEC61111

TEC61111

TEC61111

7

TEC61111

8

TEC61111

Number Cards

Use with the directions on page 133.

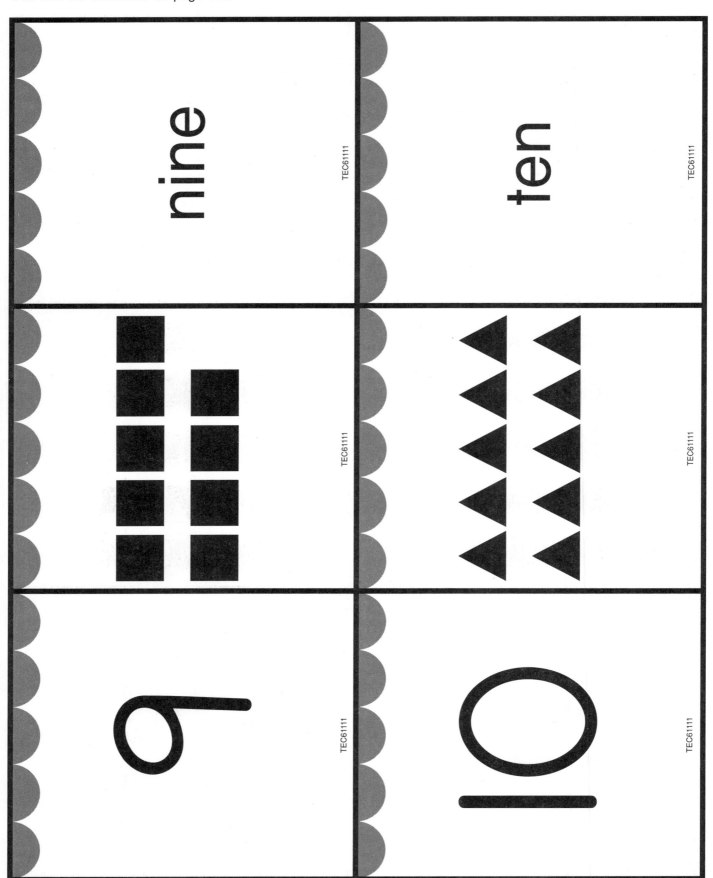

nine

ten

TEC61111

TEC61111

TEC61111

TEC61111

9

10

Everything Numbers • ©The Mailbox® Books • TEC61111

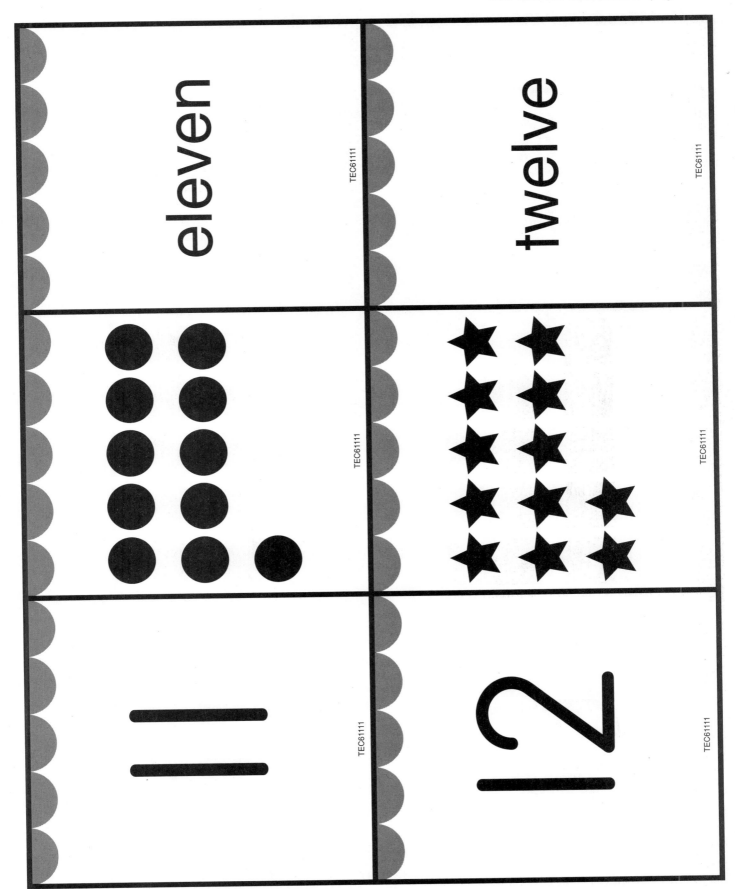

eleven

twelve

11

12

TEC61111

TEC61111

TEC61111

TEC61111

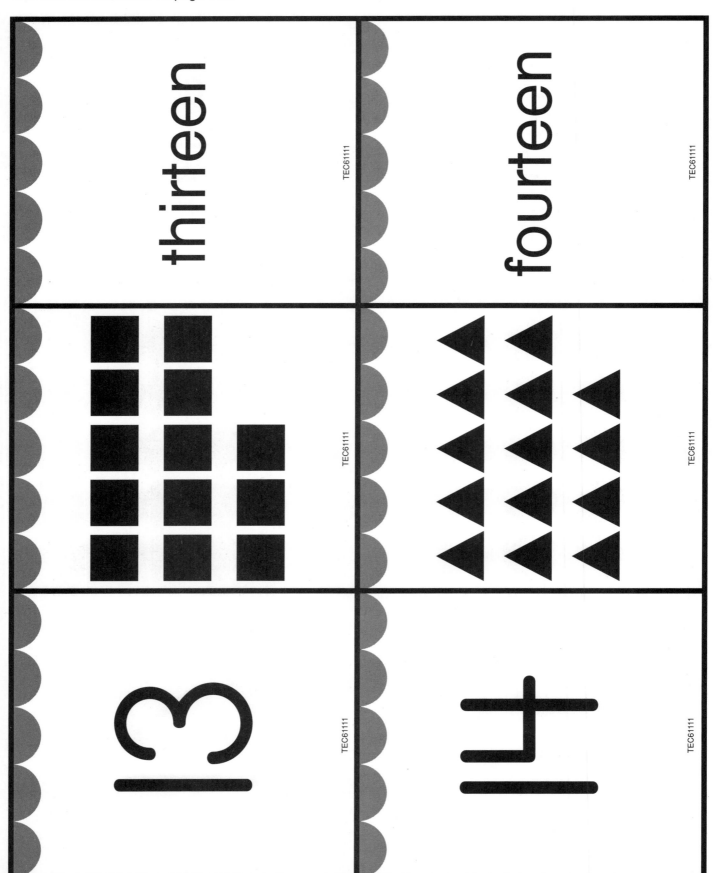

thirteen

fourteen

TEC61111

TEC61111

13

14

TEC61111

TEC61111

Everything Numbers • ©The Mailbox® Books • TEC61111

fifteen

sixteen

TEC61111

TEC61111

TEC61111

TEC61111

15

16

seventeen

eighteen

TEC61111

TEC61111

TEC61111

TEC61111

17

18

Everything Numbers • ©The Mailbox® Books • TEC61111

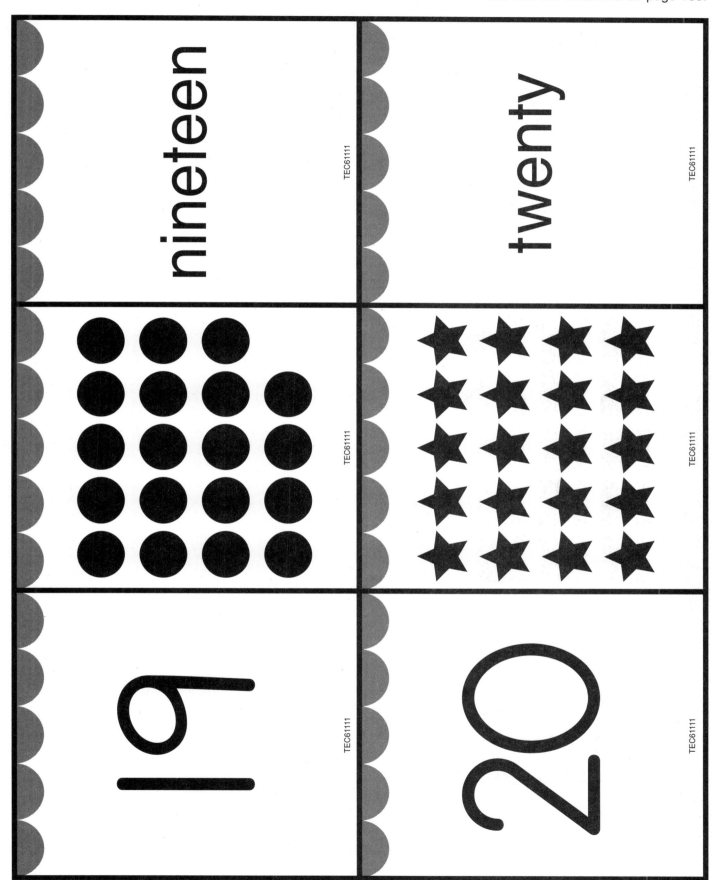

nineteen

twenty

TEC61111

TEC61111

TEC61111

TEC61111

19

20

How Many?

by

_____

Everything Numbers • ©The Mailbox® Books • TEC61111

Booklet Cover: Read the text aloud. Help the child write his name on the blank. Then have him color the artwork. Use with the booklet pages on pages 145–165.

O fish
on a dish

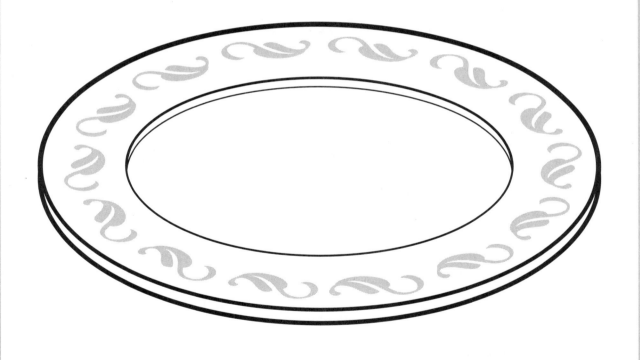

I mouse in a house

WELCOME

Everything Numbers • ©The Mailbox® Books • TEC61111

Booklet Page: Read the text aloud. Have the child verify that there is one mouse. Then have him color the page.

2 snakes eating cake

Booklet Page: Read the text aloud. Have the child verify that there are two snakes. Then have her color the page.

3 kittens
in a mitten

Booklet Page: Read the text aloud. Have the child verify that there are three kittens. Then have him color the page.

4 goats
on a boat

Booklet Page: Read the text aloud. Have the child verify that there are four goats. Then have her color the page.

5 bees
having tea

Booklet Page: Read the text aloud. Have the child verify that there are five bees. Then have him color the page.

6 bears
resting in chairs

Booklet Page: Read the text aloud. Have the child verify that there are six bears. Then have her color the page.

7 frogs
sitting on logs

Everything Numbers • ©The Mailbox® Books • TEC61111

152   **Booklet Page:** Read the text aloud. Have the child verify that there are seven frogs. Then have him color the page.

8 mice on the ice

Booklet Page: Read the text aloud. Have the child verify that there are eight mice. Then have her color the page.

9 pigs
wearing wigs

Everything Numbers • ©The Mailbox® Books • TEC61111

154   **Booklet Page:** Read the text aloud. Have the child verify that there are nine pigs. Then have him color the page.

10 rings
for the king

Everything Numbers • ©The Mailbox® Books • TEC61111

Booklet Page: Read the text aloud. Have the child verify that there are ten rings. Then have her color the page.

11 ducks
on a truck

Booklet Page: Read the text aloud. Have the child verify that there are eleven ducks. Then have him color the page.

12 foxes holding boxes

13 cats
wearing hats

Everything Numbers • ©The Mailbox® Books • TEC61111

158   **Booklet Page:** Read the text aloud. Have the child verify that there are thirteen cats. Then have him color the page.

14 bugs
under a rug

Booklet Page: Read the text aloud. Have the child verify that there are fourteen bugs. Then have her color the page.

15 sheep driving jeeps

Everything Numbers • ©The Mailbox® Books • TEC61111

Booklet Page: Read the text aloud. Have the child verify that there are fifteen sheep. Then have him color the page.

16 stars
on a car

Booklet Page: Read the text aloud. Have the child verify that there are sixteen stars. Then have her color the page.

17 snails on a trail

Everything Numbers • ©The Mailbox® Books • TEC61111

162 **Booklet Page:** Read the text aloud. Have the child verify that there are seventeen snails. Then have him color the page.

18 ants
wearing pants

Booklet Page: Read the text aloud. Have the child verify that there are eighteen ants. Then have her color the page.

19 owls
holding towels

Booklet Page: Read the text aloud. Have the child verify that there are nineteen owls. Then have him color the page.

20 dots
on a dog named Spot

Booklet Page: Read the text aloud. Have the child verify that there are 20 dots. Then have her color the page.

Beehive Counting Center
Pages 166–168

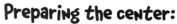

Preparing the center:
1. Copy this page and page 167 on tan construction paper.
2. Copy page 168 on yellow construction paper.
3. Cut out the cards.
4. Put each card set in a separate bag.

To practice counting, name a number. Ask the child to count out a matching number of bee cards and place them on the center mat.

To practice number identification, place a number card on the mat. Ask the child to read the number, count out a matching number of bee cards, and place the cards on the mat.

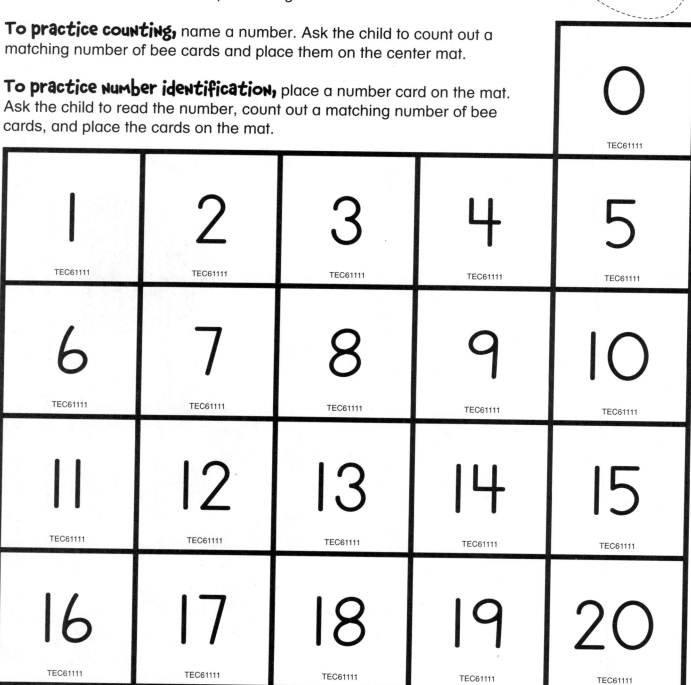

				0 TEC61111
1 TEC61111	2 TEC61111	3 TEC61111	4 TEC61111	5 TEC61111
6 TEC61111	7 TEC61111	8 TEC61111	9 TEC61111	10 TEC61111
11 TEC61111	12 TEC61111	13 TEC61111	14 TEC61111	15 TEC61111
16 TEC61111	17 TEC61111	18 TEC61111	19 TEC61111	20 TEC61111

How Many Bees?

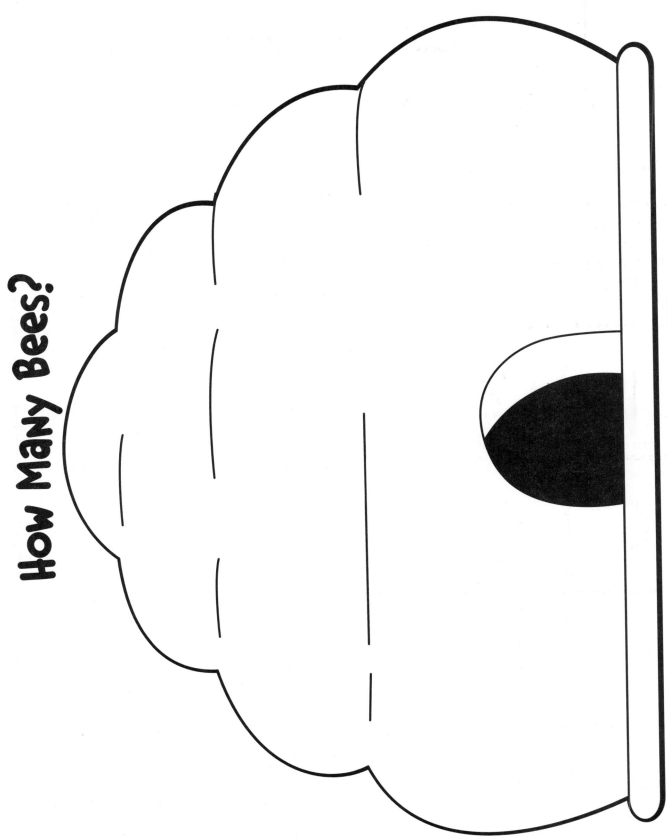

Everything Numbers • ©The Mailbox® Books • TEC61111

Note to the teacher: Use with pages 166 and 168.

Bee Cards

Use with pages 166 and 167.

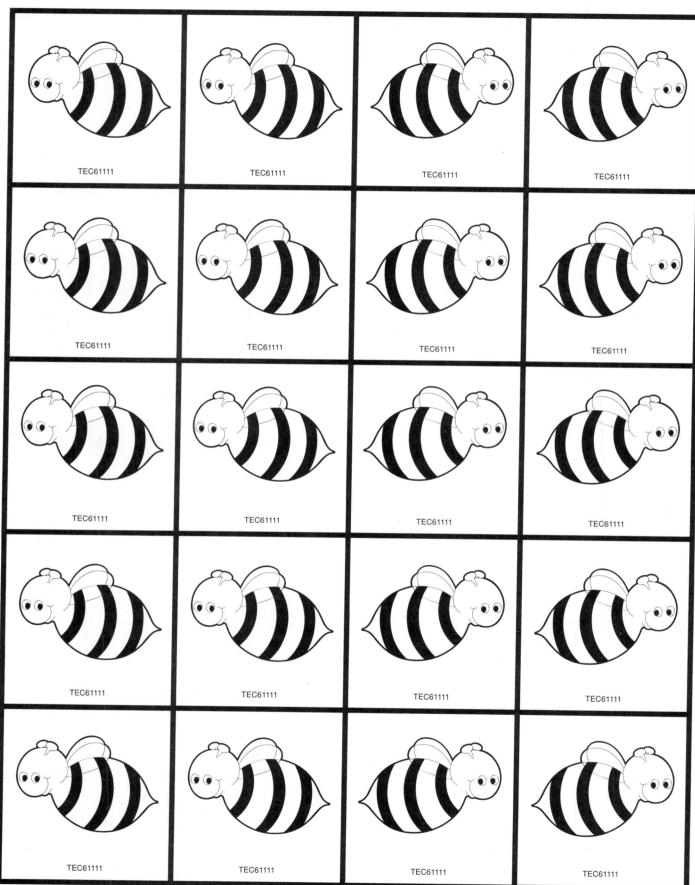

TEC61111   TEC61111   TEC61111   TEC61111

TEC61111   TEC61111   TEC61111   TEC61111

TEC61111   TEC61111   TEC61111   TEC61111

TEC61111   TEC61111   TEC61111   TEC61111

TEC61111   TEC61111   TEC61111   TEC61111

Everything Numbers • ©The Mailbox® Books • TEC61111

Bonus Activities

Number Illustrations

Center: Laminate a set of number illustrations for durability. Place several of the number pages at a center along with a supply of play dough. A child selects a number illustration. She rolls play dough into snake shapes and uses them to form the number on the page. Then she uses her index finger to trace the play dough as she names the corresponding number. She removes the play dough and repeats the activity with a different number illustration. **Number formation**

Individual: Give each child a number illustration and provide a supply of magazines and newspaper circulars. Each student cuts out examples of the number and glues them around the number on the page. **Number recognition**

Small Group: Give each child in a small group a different consecutive number illustration. The students use the numbers on their illustrations to arrange themselves in numerical order from smallest to largest. After checking the order, give each child in the group a different number illustration and repeat the activity. **Ordering numbers**

Seven.

Large Group: Place a class supply of number illustrations in a circle on the ground. Play soft music as the youngsters walk around the outside of the circle. When you stop the music, each student picks up the nearest number illustration. Then each child, in turn, identifies her number for the group. **Number identification**

Everything Numbers • ©The Mailbox® Books • TEC61111

Game Strips

Individual: Give each child a game strip. The youngster traces the numbers with a pencil. Then she uses a highlighter to trace the numbers again. Finally, she traces the numbers with a crayon. **Number formation**

Small Group: Give each student in the group a game strip. Provide magazines, blank paper, number manipulatives, an ink pad, stampers, scissors, glue, and crayons. Direct each student to use the number on his game strip to complete the tasks shown. After he completes each task, the child colors a section of his game strip. **Number sense**

Tasks:
1. Count to the number on the game strip.
2. Find the corresponding number manipulative.
3. Find an example of the number in a magazine, cut it out, and glue it to a sheet of paper.
4. Write the number on the paper.
5. Stamp a corresponding set on the paper.

Number Cards

Small Group: For each child in a group, place a number card on the floor in your group area. Place the cards that show the corresponding sets in various locations around the room. A child finds a number-set card, counts the objects on her card, and places it atop the corresponding number card. **Matching number sets to numerals**

 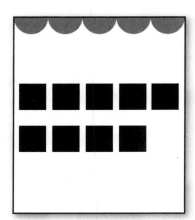

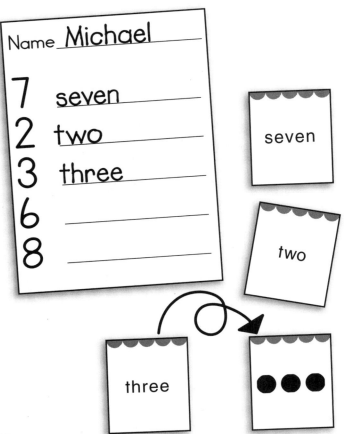

Center: Choose several number-word cards and make a recording sheet, like the one shown, with the corresponding numerals. Copy the recording sheet to make a class supply. Glue the corresponding number-set card to the back of each number-word card. Then place the cards at a center along with the recording sheets. A student finds the matching number-word card for each numeral on his paper. After checking the back of each card to verify his answer, he writes the number word beside each numeral. **Writing number words**

172

Everything Numbers • ©The Mailbox® Books • TEC61111

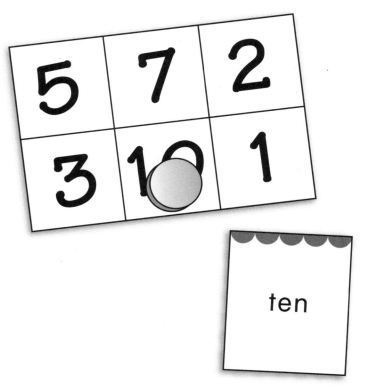

Small Group: Give each student a six-section grid and have him label each space with a different number from 1 to 10. Then give each student six game markers. Stack the number-word cards for the numbers 1 to 10 facedown. Each child, in turn, chooses a card and reads the number word aloud. Any child that has the numeral on his grid covers it with a marker. Continue in this manner until each youngster has covered all the numerals on his grid. **Number-word recognition**

ten

Partners: A youngster places the number-set cards facedown in a pile between herself and her partner. In turn, each child turns over a card from the stack and counts the number of objects shown on her card. The students compare their cards, and the child whose card has the greater number of objects keeps both cards. Play continues in this manner with the remaining cards. **Comparing number sets**

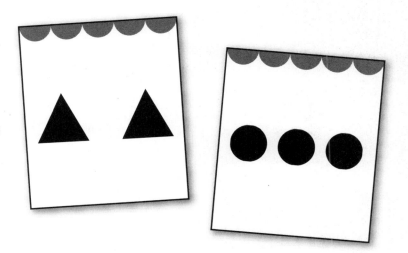

Booklet of Number Rhymes

Small Group: Have each child in a small group use his booklet of number rhymes. Display a number manipulative. Each youngster opens his booklet to the page with the corresponding number and holds it up. **Number recognition**

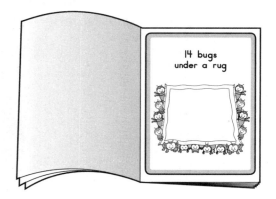

Individual: To make a class book, write the phrase from each booklet page on a separate sheet of blank paper. Give one or more of the resulting pages to each child until each page has been distributed. A youngster illustrates each phrase on her page(s). When the pages are complete, stack them in order and bind them between two construction paper covers. **Counting**

Everything Numbers • ©The Mailbox® Books • TEC61111

Individual: For an alternate version of the booklet, a youngster colors the illustrations on each booklet page. Then she makes a cover similar to the one shown. She stacks her pages in reverse order, from 20 to 1, beneath the cover and staples her booklet along the side. **Counting backward**

Beehive Counting Center

Large Group: Post a question in your group area, such as, "What will our number 'bee' today?" Each day, post a different number of bee cards below the question. During your group time, a student volunteer counts the bees to determine the number and then posts a matching number card beside the bees. **Counting**

Large Group: Designate one student to be the queen (or king) bee and give her (or him) a number card. Give each remaining child a bee card. The queen identifies the number on the card and then counts a corresponding number of worker bees by tapping each one on the shoulder. The worker bees buzz as they "fly" to a designated area of the classroom (the hive). After the class recounts the number of worker bees, give the queen a bee card and choose a new child to be the queen (or king). Have all the worker bees rejoin the class and play again. **Number identification, counting**

Buzzzz!

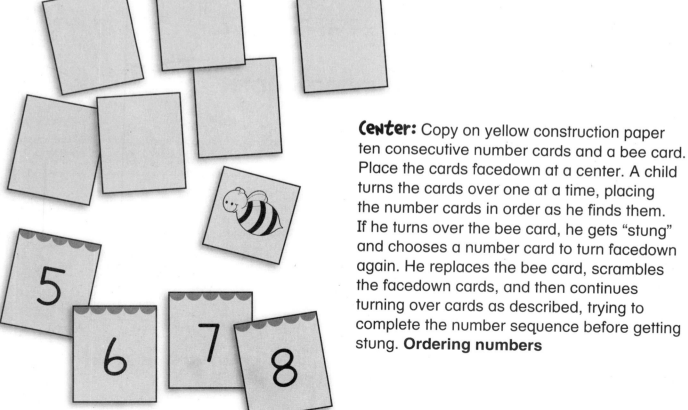

Center: Copy on yellow construction paper ten consecutive number cards and a bee card. Place the cards facedown at a center. A child turns the cards over one at a time, placing the number cards in order as he finds them. If he turns over the bee card, he gets "stung" and chooses a number card to turn facedown again. He replaces the bee card, scrambles the facedown cards, and then continues turning over cards as described, trying to complete the number sequence before getting stung. **Ordering numbers**